Do You Know About: Presidents & Prime Ministers of India 1947 - 2024

Aryak Singh Chauhan

Published by Aryak Singh Chauhan, 2024.

Do You Know About: Presidents & Prime Ministers of India 1947 - 2024

Copyright's & Disclaimer's

---

1. https://data.gov.in/sites/default/files/Gazette_Notification_OGDL.pdf

2. https://www.india.gov.in/

3. https://data.gov.in/sites/default/files/Gazette_Notification_OGDL.pdf

Table of Contents

Introduction

India's journey as an independent nation has been shaped by a series of remarkable leaders who have held the highest offices of the country—the President and the Prime Minister. These two roles, while distinct in their responsibilities and powers, have been central to the functioning of India's democracy, influencing the direction and progress of the nation over the decades. The Presidents of India, as the ceremonial heads of the state, have embodied the values and aspirations of the country, while the Prime Ministers, as the heads of the government, have steered the nation's policies and governance.

The position of the President of India was established with the country's transition to a republic in 1950. The President serves as the supreme commander of the armed forces and represents the unity and integrity of the nation. Although the role is largely ceremonial, the President's influence extends to various constitutional responsibilities, including the power to grant pardons, the appointment of key officials, and the ability to send back bills for reconsideration by the Parliament.

The Presidents of India have come from diverse backgrounds, bringing their unique experiences and perspectives to the office. From Dr. Rajendra Prasad, the first President who was deeply involved in the freedom struggle, to Droupadi Murmu, the first tribal woman to hold the office, each President has contributed to the shaping of modern India.

On the other hand, the Prime Minister is the chief executive of the country, responsible for running the government and implementing policies. The Prime Minister is the leader of the ruling party or coalition in the Parliament and is primarily responsible for the day-to-day administration of the government. The role of the Prime Minister has evolved over time, with each leader bringing their own style and priorities to the office. Jawaharlal Nehru, the first Prime Minister of India, laid the foundation for the country's development with his vision of a secular, socialist, and democratic republic. Subsequent Prime Ministers have navigated India through various challenges, from economic reforms to international diplomacy, from internal security issues to technological advancements.

This book, "Do You Know About: Presidents & Prime Ministers of India 1947 To 2024," is an attempt to provide readers with a concise yet comprehensive overview of the lives and contributions of the individuals who have held these esteemed offices. Each chapter is dedicated to a specific President or Prime Minister, offering insights into their early life, education, struggles, and the circumstances that led them to the highest offices in the country. The book also highlights their major contributions during their tenure, providing a balanced view of their achievements and challenges.

Understanding the lives of these leaders is not just about recognizing their individual contributions; it is also about appreciating the broader context in which they operated. India has faced numerous challenges since its independence, including partition, wars, economic crises, and social upheavals. The Presidents and Prime Ministers have played critical roles in navigating these challenges, making decisions that have had far-reaching consequences for the nation and its people. Their legacies are etched in the history of India, and their stories continue to inspire and guide future generations.

As you delve into the chapters of this book, you will discover the human side of these leaders—their aspirations, their struggles, and their triumphs. You will learn about Dr. Rajendra Prasad's dedication to the nation during its formative years, Dr. A. P. J. Abdul Kalam's vision for a developed India, and Narendra Modi's drive for economic and social transformation, among others. You will also encounter stories of resilience, such as Indira Gandhi's leadership during challenging times, and of innovation, like P. V. Narasimha Rao's role in liberalizing the Indian economy.

This book is not just a collection of biographies; it is a reflection of India's journey over the past seven decades. It celebrates the diversity of leadership that has guided the country, the visionaries who have dreamed big for India, and the pragmatists who have turned those dreams into reality. It is a tribute to the men and women who have dedicated their lives to the service of the nation, and in doing so, have left an indelible mark on the history of India.

As you read through the lives of these Presidents and Prime Ministers, you will gain a deeper understanding of the challenges and responsibilities that come with leadership in a vast and diverse country like India. You will also come to appreciate the significance of these roles in maintaining the democratic fabric of the nation. We hope this book will not only inform but also inspire you, just as the stories of these leaders have inspired millions of Indians over the years.

Welcome to a journey through the corridors of Indian history, seen through the lives of those who have shaped its destiny.

Part I
Presidents of India

Chapter 1:
Dr. Rajendra Prasad (1950–1962)

DR. RAJENDRA PRASAD was not only the first President of India but also one of the most respected figures in the country's history. His life and legacy are a testament to his unwavering dedication to the nation, his deep commitment to the principles of truth and justice, and his ability to lead with humility and integrity.

Birth and Early Life

DR. RAJENDRA PRASAD was born on December 3, 1884, in the village of Ziradei, in the Siwan district of Bihar. His family was deeply religious, and this spiritual environment influenced his upbringing. His father, Mahadev Sahai, was a scholar of Sanskrit and Persian, while his mother, Kamleshwari Devi, was a devout woman who instilled strong values in her children. Rajendra Prasad showed exceptional promise from a young age, excelling in his studies and displaying a keen intellect.

Education

RAJENDRA PRASAD'S ACADEMIC journey began in the rural schools of Bihar, but his thirst for knowledge soon took him to the prestigious Calcutta Presidency College, where he studied English, History, and Political Science. His brilliance as a student was evident when he topped the entrance exam for the University of Calcutta, earning a scholarship. He later pursued a law degree, completing his education with a Doctorate in Law from the same university. This solid academic foundation laid the groundwork for his future role in India's struggle for independence and in shaping the newly formed republic.

Struggle for Independence

DR. RAJENDRA PRASAD was deeply influenced by Mahatma Gandhi's philosophy and became an ardent follower of his principles of non-violence and civil disobedience. His involvement in the Indian National Congress marked the beginning of a long and illustrious political career. He played a pivotal role in various movements, including the Champaran Satyagraha in 1917, where he worked alongside Gandhi to address the grievances of indigo farmers in Bihar. His leadership in this movement not only brought him national recognition but also solidified his commitment to the cause of Indian independence.

Throughout the freedom struggle, Dr. Prasad was imprisoned multiple times by the British authorities, but his resolve remained unshaken. He served as the President of the Indian National Congress during some of the most challenging periods, including the Quit India Movement in 1942. His ability to lead with calm and determination during these turbulent times earned him the respect and admiration of his peers and the nation.

Success and Role as President

AFTER INDIA GAINED independence in 1947, Dr. Rajendra Prasad was elected as the President of the Constituent Assembly, where he played a crucial role in drafting the Constitution of India. His deep understanding of law and his commitment to democratic principles made him an ideal candidate for this position. When India became a republic on January 26, 1950, Dr. Rajendra Prasad was unanimously elected as the first President of India, a position he held with distinction for 12 years, making him the longest-serving President in Indian history.

As President, Dr. Prasad maintained the dignity of the office while ensuring that he remained accessible to the people. He believed in the importance of being a moral compass for the nation and often intervened in matters where he felt that the principles of justice and fairness were at stake. His tenure saw India navigate through its early challenges as a republic, including the integration of princely states, the linguistic reorganization of states, and the challenges posed by external aggression.

Later Years and Death

DR. RAJENDRA PRASAD retired from public life in 1962, after serving two terms as President. He spent his later years in the quietude of his ancestral home in Bihar, engaging in writing and reflection. His autobiography, "Atmakatha," offers a deep insight into his life, thoughts, and the philosophy that guided him. He also penned several other works, including "India Divided," which remains a significant contribution to Indian political literature.

Dr. Rajendra Prasad passed away on February 28, 1963, leaving behind a legacy of selfless service and unwavering commitment to the nation. He was posthumously awarded the Bharat Ratna, India's highest civilian honor, in recognition of his immense contributions to the country.

Major Contributions During His Tenure

DURING HIS TENURE AS President, Dr. Rajendra Prasad's contributions were pivotal in establishing the foundations of India's democratic institutions. He played a crucial role in ensuring that the newly drafted Constitution was implemented effectively and that the principles of democracy, secularism, and social justice were upheld. His interactions with the Prime Ministers of the time, especially Jawaharlal Nehru, were marked by mutual respect and a shared vision for the nation, even though they occasionally had differences of opinion.

Dr. Prasad also emphasized the importance of education and worked towards improving the educational infrastructure in the country. He believed that education was the key to India's progress and was instrumental in the establishment of various educational institutions. His speeches often highlighted the need for a strong moral and ethical foundation in the country's development.

In conclusion, Dr. Rajendra Prasad's life is a shining example of dedication, humility, and integrity. His contributions to India's freedom struggle, his role in shaping the republic, and his leadership as the first President of India continue to inspire generations of Indians. He remains a revered figure in Indian history, embodying the ideals of service and commitment to the nation.

Chapter 2

Dr. Sarvepalli Radhakrishnan (1962–1967)

DR. SARVEPALLI RADHAKRISHNAN, the second President of India, was a distinguished philosopher, scholar, and statesman. His journey from humble beginnings to becoming one of the most respected figures in Indian history is a story of intellectual brilliance, dedication to education, and deep commitment to the nation's values.

Birth and Early Life

DR. SARVEPALLI RADHAKRISHNAN was born on September 5, 1888, in the small village of Tiruttani, in present-day Tamil Nadu. His family was not wealthy, and his father, Sarvepalli Veeraswami, worked as a subordinate revenue official. Despite the family's modest means, Radhakrishnan was encouraged to pursue education from an early age. His mother, Sitamma, played a significant role in nurturing his spiritual and ethical values, which would later influence his philosophical outlook.

Radhakrishnan's early education took place in Christian missionary institutions, where he excelled in his studies. His exceptional intelligence and keen interest in religion and philosophy became evident during his school years, and these interests would shape his future career.

Education

DR. RADHAKRISHNAN'S academic journey began with a scholarship to study at the Madras Christian College, where he earned his bachelor's degree with honors in philosophy. He continued his education at the same institution, completing his master's degree in philosophy. It was during this period that he delved deeply into the study of Indian philosophy, particularly the works of classical Indian thinkers like Adi Shankaracharya and Ramanuja. Radhakrishnan's thesis on "The Ethics of the Vedanta and Its Metaphysical Presuppositions" earned him widespread acclaim and marked the beginning of his illustrious academic career.

After completing his education, Radhakrishnan began teaching philosophy at the Madras Presidency College and later at the University of Mysore. His lectures were known for their depth and clarity, and he quickly gained recognition as one of India's leading scholars of philosophy. In 1921, he was appointed as a professor of philosophy at the University of Calcutta, where he continued to teach and write on various philosophical subjects, bridging Eastern and Western thought.

Philosophical Contributions and Academic Achievements

DR. RADHAKRISHNAN'S contributions to philosophy were profound and far-reaching. He was a key figure in interpreting Indian philosophy for the Western world, making complex ideas accessible and relevant to a global audience. His works, including "Indian Philosophy," "The Philosophy of the Upanishads," and "Eastern Religions and Western Thought," are considered seminal in the field of comparative religion and philosophy.

Radhakrishnan's philosophy emphasized the unity of all religions and the underlying spiritual oneness of humanity. He believed that true religion transcends dogma and ritual, focusing instead on the direct experience of the divine. His writings promoted a vision of global peace and harmony, grounded in the spiritual traditions of India.

In recognition of his scholarly contributions, Radhakrishnan was appointed to several prestigious positions, including the Spalding Professor of Eastern Religions and Ethics at the University of Oxford. He was also invited to deliver the Hibbert Lectures, a significant honor in the field of religious studies.

Political Involvement and Role as Vice President

DR. RADHAKRISHNAN'S academic achievements naturally led him to the international stage, where he represented India at various forums, including UNESCO and the United Nations. His eloquence, deep knowledge, and commitment to world peace made him a respected figure in global diplomacy.

In 1952, following India's independence, Dr. Radhakrishnan was appointed as the first Vice President of India. In this role, he presided over the Rajya Sabha (Council of States) and provided intellectual and moral guidance to the nation during its formative years. His tenure as Vice President was marked by his ability to navigate complex political situations with wisdom and tact, earning him the respect of both political leaders and the public.

Presidency and Contributions

DR. RADHAKRISHNAN WAS elected as the second President of India in 1962, succeeding Dr. Rajendra Prasad. His presidency was characterized by his focus on education, ethics, and international relations. Although the role of the President in India is largely ceremonial, Dr. Radhakrishnan brought a new level of dignity and intellectual stature to the office.

One of his most significant contributions as President was his emphasis on education as a means of national development. He believed that education should be rooted in India's cultural and spiritual heritage while also embracing modern scientific and technological advancements. To honor his contributions to education, his birthday, September 5th, is celebrated as Teacher's Day in India, a tradition that continues to this day.

During his presidency, India faced several challenges, including the Indo-China War of 1962. Dr. Radhakrishnan played a crucial role in boosting the morale of the nation during this difficult time, using his speeches to inspire a sense of unity and resilience among the Indian people.

Later Years and Death

AFTER COMPLETING HIS term as President in 1967, Dr. Radhakrishnan retired from public life, spending his later years in quiet reflection and writing. He continued to be an influential voice on matters of philosophy, religion, and education until his death on April 17, 1975.

Dr. Radhakrishnan's legacy is not only as a President and philosopher but also as a teacher who inspired generations of students and scholars. His life exemplified the values of intellectual curiosity, spiritual depth, and ethical leadership. He was posthumously awarded the Bharat Ratna, India's highest civilian honor, in 1954, in recognition of his monumental contributions to Indian thought and society.

Major Contributions During His Tenure

DURING HIS TENURE AS President, Dr. Radhakrishnan was instrumental in promoting India's image as a peace-loving nation committed to the principles of democracy and non-violence. His speeches and writings during this period emphasized the need for global cooperation and understanding, especially in the context of the Cold War.

Domestically, Dr. Radhakrishnan advocated for educational reforms that would make India a leader in science and technology while preserving its rich cultural heritage. His vision for education continues to influence policies and initiatives in India today.

In summary, Dr. Sarvepalli Radhakrishnan's life was a remarkable journey of intellectual achievement, spiritual exploration, and dedicated service to the nation. His tenure as President of India was marked by his unwavering commitment to education, ethics, and international harmony. He remains a towering figure in Indian history, whose legacy continues to inspire and guide future generations.

Chapter 3:
Dr. Zakir Husain (1967–1969)

DR. ZAKIR HUSAIN WAS the third President of India and the first Muslim to hold this esteemed office. A scholar, educationist, and visionary, Dr. Husain's life was dedicated to the pursuit of knowledge, the promotion of education, and the upliftment of the underprivileged. His tenure as President, though brief, left a lasting impact on the nation, particularly in the fields of education and social reform.

Birth and Early Life

DR. ZAKIR HUSAIN WAS born on February 8, 1897, in Hyderabad, in what was then the Nizam's Dominion, now in the Indian state of Telangana. He belonged to a family known for its scholarly traditions. His father, Fida Husain Khan, was a respected lawyer, and his mother, Naznin Begum, was a deeply religious woman. Dr. Husain lost his father at a young age, and his mother had to move with her children to the family's ancestral home in Qaimganj, a small town in Uttar Pradesh.

Despite these early hardships, Dr. Zakir Husain's passion for learning was evident from a young age. He attended Islamia High School in Etawah and later enrolled at the Muhammadan Anglo-Oriental College in Aligarh, which was later to become the Aligarh Muslim University (AMU). His time at Aligarh was formative, not only in terms of his academic achievements but also in shaping his future as an educationist and nationalist.

Education

DR. ZAKIR HUSAIN WAS a brilliant student, excelling in his studies and developing a deep interest in literature, philosophy, and social sciences. He completed his Bachelor's degree at Aligarh with honors and later pursued a Master's degree in Economics. His academic prowess earned him a scholarship to study in Germany, where he enrolled at the University of Berlin. There, he obtained a doctorate in Economics, further solidifying his reputation as a scholar of international standing.

During his time in Germany, Dr. Husain was deeply influenced by the ideas of Western education and philosophy. However, he remained committed to his Indian roots and was determined to use his education for the betterment of his country. His exposure to the German educational system, particularly its emphasis on vocational and technical education, had a lasting impact on his vision for India's educational future.

Struggle for Independence and Contributions to Education

UPON RETURNING TO INDIA in the 1920s, Dr. Zakir Husain became actively involved in the Indian independence movement. He believed that education was a critical tool in the struggle against colonialism and was instrumental in establishing the Jamia Millia Islamia in 1920, a nationalist educational institution that sought to provide an alternative to British-run schools. As one of the founding members and later the Vice-Chancellor of Jamia Millia Islamia, Dr. Husain dedicated his life to building an educational system that combined modern scientific knowledge with India's rich cultural heritage.

Under his leadership, Jamia Millia Islamia grew into a prominent institution that not only provided quality education but also promoted the ideals of self-reliance, social justice, and communal harmony. Dr. Husain's work at Jamia earned him widespread recognition as an educationist who believed in the power of education to transform society.

In addition to his work at Jamia Millia Islamia, Dr. Zakir Husain was also involved in various other educational initiatives. He served on several educational committees and commissions, where he advocated for reforms that would make education more accessible and relevant to the needs of the Indian population. His contributions to the development of education in India were recognized by the government, and he was awarded the Padma Vibhushan in 1954.

Role as Vice President and Presidency

IN 1957, DR. ZAKIR Husain was appointed as the Vice President of India, a role in which he served with distinction for ten years. As

Vice President, he also served as the ex-officio Chairman of the Rajya Sabha, the upper house of India's Parliament. His tenure was marked by his efforts to promote educational and cultural initiatives and to encourage a spirit of tolerance and understanding among India's diverse population.

In 1967, Dr. Zakir Husain was elected as the President of India, becoming the first Muslim to hold this position. His election was seen as a symbol of India's secularism and its commitment to promoting unity in diversity. As President, Dr. Husain continued to champion the cause of education, and he used his office to promote the values of peace, tolerance, and social justice.

Major Contributions During His Tenure

DR. ZAKIR HUSAIN'S presidency, though brief, was marked by his emphasis on the importance of education as a means of national development. He believed that education was not just about acquiring knowledge, but about building character and fostering a sense of social responsibility. He often spoke about the need for an education system that would produce citizens who were not only knowledgeable but also compassionate and committed to the welfare of society.

During his tenure, Dr. Husain also worked to strengthen India's cultural and intellectual ties with other countries. He was a firm believer in the idea that India could learn much from the experiences of other nations, while also sharing its own rich cultural heritage with the world. His efforts to promote cultural exchange and international cooperation were well-received, and he was respected as a statesman of great wisdom and integrity.

Death and Legacy

TRAGICALLY, DR. ZAKIR Husain's tenure as President was cut short when he passed away suddenly on May 3, 1969, while still in office. His death was a great loss to the nation, and he was mourned by people from all walks of life. In recognition of his contributions to the country, Dr. Husain was posthumously awarded the Bharat Ratna, India's highest civilian honor.

Dr. Zakir Husain's legacy lives on through the institutions he helped build and the values he espoused. Jamia Millia Islamia stands as a testament to his vision of an education system that is inclusive, progressive, and rooted in the values of justice and equality. His life and work continue to inspire educators, students, and leaders in India and around the world.

Conclusion

DR. ZAKIR HUSAIN'S life was a shining example of dedication to education, social reform, and national unity. His contributions to the field of education, both as an administrator and as a scholar, have left an indelible mark on India. As President, he brought to the office a deep sense of responsibility, humility, and a commitment to the welfare of all Indians. His tenure may have been brief, but his impact on the nation was profound, and his legacy continues to inspire future generations.

Chapter 4:
Varahagiri Venkata Giri (1969–1974)

VARAHAGIRI VENKATA Giri, popularly known as V. V. Giri, was the fourth President of India, serving from 1969 to 1974. A man of humble origins, Giri rose through the ranks of Indian politics, earning a reputation as a tireless advocate for workers' rights and a staunch supporter of social justice. His tenure as President was marked by significant political events, including the consolidation of Indira Gandhi's power and the deepening of democratic institutions in India.

Birth and Early Life

V. V. GIRI WAS BORN on August 10, 1894, in Berhampur, a town in the Ganjam district of the Madras Presidency, now part of Odisha. He came from a Telugu-speaking Brahmin family with strong nationalist leanings. His father, V. V. Jogayya Pantulu, was an advocate and a prominent public figure who actively participated in the Indian independence movement. From a young age, Giri was exposed to the ideas of nationalism and social reform, which greatly influenced his future career.

Education

GIRI BEGAN HIS EDUCATION in Berhampur, attending local schools before moving to Dublin, Ireland, where he studied law at University College Dublin. During his time in Dublin, Giri became involved in the Irish nationalist movement, which was fighting for independence from British rule. His experiences in Ireland deepened his commitment to India's own struggle for freedom. After completing his studies, Giri returned to India, where he joined the legal profession but soon became deeply involved in the labor movement.

Involvement in the Labor Movement and Freedom Struggle

GIRI'S INVOLVEMENT in the labor movement began in the early 1920s when he joined the All India Trade Union Congress (AITUC), one of the oldest trade unions in India. He quickly emerged as a leading figure in the labor movement, advocating for the rights of workers and organizing strikes to demand better wages and working conditions. Giri's work in the labor movement earned him the respect of workers across India and established him as a champion of social justice.

Simultaneously, Giri was an active participant in the Indian freedom struggle. He was a staunch supporter of Mahatma Gandhi's principles of non-violence and civil disobedience and played a key role in organizing workers to participate in the freedom movement. Giri was arrested several times by the British authorities for his involvement in protests and strikes, but his commitment to the cause remained unwavering.

Political Career and Role as Vice President

AFTER INDIA GAINED independence in 1947, Giri's political career continued to flourish. He served in various capacities, including as the Minister of Labor in the interim government and later as the Governor of Uttar Pradesh, Kerala, and Mysore. His deep understanding of labor issues and his commitment to social justice made him a respected figure in Indian politics.

In 1967, Giri was elected as the Vice President of India, a position in which he served with distinction. As Vice President, he also held the office of Chairman of the Rajya Sabha, where he played a crucial role in guiding legislative debates and maintaining decorum in the upper house of Parliament. His experience in both labor and politics gave him a unique perspective, and he used his position to advocate for policies that promoted social and economic equality.

Presidency and Major Contributions

V. V. GIRI'S ASCENT to the presidency in 1969 was marked by political intrigue and controversy. After the sudden death of President Zakir Husain, Giri, who was serving as Vice President at the time, was appointed Acting President. The subsequent presidential election saw Giri contest as an independent candidate, supported by Prime Minister Indira Gandhi against the official Congress candidate, Neelam Sanjiva Reddy. Giri's victory in the election was a significant political event, as it underscored the growing rift within the Congress Party and marked the beginning of Indira Gandhi's consolidation of power.

As President, Giri played a largely ceremonial role, but his tenure was nonetheless significant for several reasons. One of his most notable contributions was his support for Indira Gandhi during a period of intense political turmoil. This included the controversial decision to nationalize 14 major banks in 1969, a move that was seen as a step towards socialism and was intended to bring about greater economic equality. Giri's support for this policy reflected his long-standing commitment to social justice and his belief in the need for state intervention to address economic disparities.

Giri's presidency also coincided with the abolition of privy purses in 1971, a move that ended the financial privileges of the former rulers of the princely states. This decision was seen as a step towards strengthening the democratic fabric of India and reducing the influence of feudal elements in the country.

Later Years and Legacy

AFTER COMPLETING HIS term as President in 1974, V. V. Giri retired from active politics, spending his remaining years in relative quietude. He remained a respected figure in Indian public life, known for his integrity, simplicity, and dedication to the cause of social justice. Giri passed away on June 24, 1980, at the age of 85.

Giri's legacy is particularly significant in the context of India's labor movement. His efforts to improve the working conditions of Indian laborers and his role in shaping labor policy in the early years of India's independence continue to be remembered and respected. In recognition of his contributions to the nation, Giri was awarded the Bharat Ratna, India's highest civilian honor, in 1975.

Conclusion

V. V. GIRI'S LIFE AND career are a testament to his unwavering commitment to the principles of social justice, equality, and national unity. As President of India, he played a crucial role during a period of significant political and economic change, helping to steer the country through challenging times with dignity and foresight. His contributions to the labor movement and his dedication to the welfare of the working class remain an enduring part of his legacy.

FAKHRUDDIN ALI AHMED was the fifth President of India, serving from 1974 until his untimely death in 1977. His tenure was one of the most politically charged periods in India's history, marked by the declaration of the Emergency by Prime Minister Indira Gandhi. A lawyer by profession and a politician by passion, Ahmed's presidency was defined by his loyalty to the Prime Minister and his commitment to the nation's constitutional framework, albeit during a tumultuous time.

Birth and Early Life

FAKHRUDDIN ALI AHMED was born on May 13, 1905, in the Hauz Qazi area of Old Delhi. He belonged to an illustrious Assamese Muslim family with a strong tradition of public service. His father, Col. Zalnur Ali Ahmed, was a noted physician, and his mother, Rabia Begum, was a woman of deep religious convictions. The family hailed from Assam, a region that played a significant role in shaping Ahmed's early worldview and later his political career.

Education

AHMED'S EARLY EDUCATION took place at the Government High School in Gonda, Uttar Pradesh. He later moved to Delhi, where he attended St. Stephen's College, one of the most prestigious institutions in the country. After completing his graduation, Ahmed went to England to study law at St Catharine's College, Cambridge. During his time in England, he was called to the Bar at the Inner Temple in London, one of the four Inns of Court that trained barristers.

While in England, Ahmed came into contact with several Indian nationalists, including Jawaharlal Nehru. These interactions, combined with the political environment in Europe, deepened his commitment to the cause of Indian independence. Upon returning to India, Ahmed began practicing law in Assam and quickly became involved in the Indian National Congress and the freedom struggle.

Political Career and Struggle for Independence

FAKHRUDDIN ALI AHMED was drawn to the Indian National Congress, where he worked closely with leaders like Jawaharlal Nehru and Maulana Abul Kalam Azad. His deep sense of nationalism and his legal acumen made him a valuable asset to the party. He participated actively in the freedom movement, particularly in Assam, and was arrested several times by the British authorities for his involvement in the Quit India Movement of 1942.

After India gained independence in 1947, Ahmed continued his political career, holding various important positions within the Congress Party. He was elected to the Assam Legislative Assembly and later to the Lok Sabha, where he served as a Member of Parliament for several terms. Ahmed held various ministerial portfolios, including Agriculture, Cooperation, Education, and Industrial Development, under Prime Ministers Nehru, Lal Bahadur Shastri, and Indira Gandhi.

Presidency and the Emergency

IN 1974, FAKHRUDDIN Ali Ahmed was elected as the President of India, becoming the second Muslim to hold the office after Dr. Zakir Husain. His presidency, however, is most remembered for the role he played during the Emergency, a 21-month period from 1975 to 1977, when Prime Minister Indira Gandhi assumed near-total control over the government.

The Emergency was declared on June 25, 1975, by Prime Minister Indira Gandhi, citing internal disturbances as the reason. Fakhruddin Ali Ahmed, as President, signed the proclamation of the Emergency without hesitation, an act that has been a subject of much debate and criticism. Critics argue that Ahmed, as the custodian of the Constitution, should have questioned or resisted the move, but his decision was consistent with the convention of acting on the advice of the Prime Minister.

During the Emergency, civil liberties were suspended, political opponents were arrested, and press censorship was imposed. The period remains one of the most controversial in Indian history. Ahmed's role during this time was seen as that of a constitutional figurehead who, despite the extraordinary circumstances, adhered to the letter of the Constitution.

Major Contributions and Controversies

FAKHRUDDIN ALI AHMED'S tenure as President is often overshadowed by the Emergency. However, it is important to note that his career before the presidency was marked by significant contributions to Indian politics and governance. As a minister, he played a key role in implementing agricultural and educational reforms, which had a lasting impact on the country.

Despite his contributions, Ahmed's legacy is inevitably tied to the Emergency. His decision to sign the proclamation and other ordinances that curtailed fundamental rights has been a point of contention among historians and political analysts. While some argue that he had little choice given the political climate, others believe that he could have taken a stand against the actions of the government.

Death and Legacy

FAKHRUDDIN ALI AHMED'S presidency was cut short by his sudden death on February 11, 1977. He passed away while still in office, making him the second Indian President to die in office after Dr. Zakir Husain. His death came just months before the end of the Emergency, and India soon returned to normalcy with the restoration of democratic processes.

Ahmed's legacy is complex. On one hand, he is remembered as a leader who served his country with dedication and who held important ministerial positions during critical periods of India's history. On the other hand, his role during the Emergency continues to spark debate. Despite this, Fakhruddin Ali Ahmed remains a significant figure in India's political history, representing the challenges and responsibilities of upholding constitutional duties in times of crisis.

Conclusion

FAKHRUDDIN ALI AHMED'S life was marked by his dedication to public service, his commitment to the Indian National Congress, and his deep belief in the principles of democracy and secularism. His presidency came at a time of great political upheaval, and his actions during the Emergency have left a lasting impact on how the role of the President is viewed in India's democratic framework. While his tenure is often seen through the lens of the Emergency, it is important to remember his broader contributions to India's political and social landscape.

Chapter 6:
Neelam Sanjiva Reddy (1977–1982)

NEELAM SANJIVA REDDY was the sixth President of India, serving from 1977 to 1982. His presidency was notable for its context within the post-Emergency period, a time when India's democracy was being restored after a significant crisis. Known for his humility, integrity, and simplicity, Reddy was the first President of India to be elected unopposed, reflecting the widespread respect he commanded across the political spectrum.

Birth and Early Life

NEELAM SANJIVA REDDY was born on May 19, 1913, in Illur, a small village in the Anantapur district of the Madras Presidency, which is now in Andhra Pradesh. He came from a modest agricultural family, and his early life was deeply rooted in the rural traditions and culture of South India. Despite the challenges of growing up in a rural setting, Reddy was determined to pursue an education and contribute to the national cause.

Education

REDDY BEGAN HIS EDUCATION at the Theosophical High School in Adyar, Madras (now Chennai), before moving on to the prestigious Government Arts College in Anantapur. His early exposure to the teachings of Mahatma Gandhi and the nationalist movement had a profound influence on him, leading him to become actively involved in the freedom struggle at a young age. He eventually left college to join the Indian independence movement, dedicating himself to the cause of a free India.

Involvement in the Freedom Struggle

SANJIVA REDDY'S POLITICAL journey began in earnest when he joined the Indian National Congress in the early 1930s. He quickly rose through the ranks, thanks to his dedication and organizational skills. He participated in the Civil Disobedience Movement and the Quit India Movement, both of which led to his imprisonment by the British authorities. His commitment to the freedom struggle earned him the trust and admiration of senior Congress leaders, including Jawaharlal Nehru and Sardar Vallabhbhai Patel.

Reddy's leadership qualities were recognized early on, and he became a prominent figure in the Andhra Pradesh Congress. He was instrumental in mobilizing the masses in the region and played a key role in the fight against British colonial rule. His efforts were particularly focused on rural areas, where he worked to empower farmers and the working class, reflecting his deep-rooted belief in social justice and equality.

Political Career After Independence

AFTER INDIA GAINED independence in 1947, Sanjiva Reddy continued his political career with the Indian National Congress. He was elected to the Constituent Assembly of India, where he contributed to the drafting of the Indian Constitution. Reddy was also a member of the first Lok Sabha, the lower house of India's Parliament, representing the Anantapur constituency.

Reddy's political acumen and commitment to public service led to his appointment as the Chief Minister of Andhra Pradesh in 1956, a position he held until 1960. During his tenure, he focused on the development of the state, particularly in the areas of agriculture, irrigation, and education. His work as Chief Minister laid the foundation for Andhra Pradesh's future growth and earned him a reputation as an able and honest administrator.

Following his term as Chief Minister, Reddy held several important positions in the Indian government. He served as the Minister of Steel and Mines and later as the Minister of Transport and Civil Aviation under Prime Ministers Nehru and Lal Bahadur Shastri. His contributions in these roles were significant, particularly in the development of India's infrastructure and the promotion of industrial growth.

Presidency and Major Contributions

IN 1977, NEELAM SANJIVA Reddy was elected as the President of India, becoming the first and only President to be elected unopposed. His election came in the aftermath of the Emergency, a period of political turmoil and authoritarian rule under Prime Minister Indira Gandhi. The Janata Party, which had come to power after defeating Indira Gandhi's Congress Party in the 1977 general elections, supported Reddy's candidacy, seeing him as a leader who could help restore faith in India's democratic institutions.

As President, Reddy played a crucial role in stabilizing the country's political environment. He was known for his impartiality, fairness, and adherence to constitutional principles. His tenure was marked by several important developments, including the transition of power from the Janata Party to Indira Gandhi's Congress Party after the 1980 general elections.

Reddy's presidency was also notable for his emphasis on the importance of maintaining the dignity and integrity of the office. He believed that the President's role was to act as a neutral and non-partisan figure, ensuring that the Constitution was upheld and that the government functioned within the bounds of the law. Reddy's commitment to these principles helped to strengthen India's democracy during a critical period.

Later Years and Legacy

AFTER COMPLETING HIS term as President in 1982, Neelam Sanjiva Reddy retired from active politics. He returned to his hometown in Andhra Pradesh, where he lived a simple and peaceful life, away from the limelight. Despite his withdrawal from public life, Reddy remained a respected figure in Indian politics, admired for his integrity, humility, and dedication to public service.

Reddy passed away on June 1, 1996, at the age of 83. His death was mourned by leaders across the political spectrum, who remembered him as a leader who had served the nation with distinction and honor.

Conclusion

NEELAM SANJIVA REDDY'S life and career were marked by a deep commitment to the values of democracy, social justice, and integrity. As the sixth President of India, he played a pivotal role in restoring the nation's democratic institutions after a period of political crisis. His leadership, both as a politician and as President, was characterized by a strong sense of duty and a commitment to the welfare of the people. Reddy's legacy continues to inspire future generations of leaders, serving as a reminder of the importance of integrity and humility in public service.

GIANI ZAIL SINGH SERVED as the seventh President of India from 1982 to 1987, a period marked by both challenges and controversies. Known for his deep religious devotion, simplicity, and grassroots connection with the people, Zail Singh's presidency was one of the most eventful in Indian history. His term was characterized by major national events, including the assassination of Prime Minister

Indira Gandhi and the subsequent anti-Sikh riots, as well as the rise of militancy in Punjab.

Birth and Early Life

GIANI ZAIL SINGH WAS born on May 5, 1916, in Sandhwan, a small village in the Faridkot district of Punjab, during the British Raj. His birth name was Jarnail Singh, but he later adopted the title "Giani," which denotes a person knowledgeable in Sikh religious texts. Zail Singh's father, Kishan Singh, was a farmer, and the family lived a modest life, rooted in Sikh traditions.

From a young age, Zail Singh was deeply influenced by the teachings of Sikhism and developed a strong connection to his faith. His early education took place in religious schools, where he studied Sikh scriptures and learned the principles of his religion. The hardship and poverty he faced in his early life shaped his worldview and commitment to serving the underprivileged.

Education and Early Activism

DESPITE LIMITED FORMAL education, Zail Singh became a well-versed scholar in Sikh religious texts and earned the title of "Giani." His deep religious conviction and his passion for social justice led him to become involved in the political movements of the time, particularly the struggle for India's independence from British rule.

Zail Singh's political career began in the early 1940s when he joined the freedom struggle under the influence of prominent leaders of the Indian National Congress. He was particularly drawn to the leadership of Mahatma Gandhi and Jawaharlal Nehru. He played an active role in the Quit India Movement of 1942, which led to his imprisonment by the British authorities. His time in prison only strengthened his resolve to fight for India's independence.

Political Career After Independence

AFTER INDIA GAINED independence in 1947, Zail Singh continued his political journey with the Indian National Congress. He quickly rose through the ranks, becoming a prominent leader in Punjab. In 1949, he was appointed as the Revenue Minister of the newly formed Patiala and East Punjab States Union (PEPSU), where he worked on land reforms and the rehabilitation of refugees who had been displaced during the Partition.

Zail Singh's leadership and organizational skills were recognized, and he was elected as the Chief Minister of Punjab in 1972. As Chief Minister, he focused on infrastructure development, social welfare programs, and improving law and order in the state. His tenure was marked by efforts to uplift the marginalized sections of society, particularly in rural areas. He also played a key role in promoting communal harmony in Punjab, which was beginning to face the early signs of religious tensions.

Presidency and Major Contributions

IN 1982, ZAIL SINGH was elected as the President of India, becoming the first Sikh to hold the highest constitutional office in the country. His election was seen as a recognition of his long-standing service to the nation and his deep connection with the people. However, his presidency was not without challenges, as it coincided with one of the most turbulent periods in India's post-independence history.

One of the most significant events during Zail Singh's presidency was Operation Blue Star in June 1984. This military operation, ordered by Prime Minister Indira Gandhi, aimed to flush out militants who had taken refuge in the Golden Temple, the holiest shrine of the Sikhs, in Amritsar. The operation led to significant casualties and widespread outrage among the Sikh community, leading to a period of intense communal tension in Punjab.

Zail Singh, as President, faced a difficult situation. His loyalty to Indira Gandhi, who had appointed him, was tested against his deep-rooted Sikh identity and the sentiments of his community. The situation became even more complex when Indira Gandhi was assassinated by her Sikh bodyguards on October 31, 1984. The assassination was followed by anti-Sikh riots, where thousands of Sikhs were killed in Delhi and other parts of the country.

Zail Singh's response to these events has been the subject of much debate. While he expressed his grief and concern over the violence, his inability to prevent or stop the riots led to criticism. Some believed that as President, he should have taken a stronger stand against the government's failure to protect the Sikh community. Nonetheless, Zail Singh maintained that he did everything within his constitutional powers to address the situation.

Another critical moment during his presidency was the friction between Zail Singh and Prime Minister Rajiv Gandhi, who succeeded his mother, Indira Gandhi, after her assassination. The relationship between the President and the Prime Minister became strained over issues of constitutional authority and governance. Despite these tensions, Zail Singh chose not to act against the government, maintaining his belief in upholding the Constitution and the democratic process.

Later Years and Legacy

AFTER COMPLETING HIS term as President in 1987, Giani Zail Singh retired from active politics. He returned to Punjab, where he continued to be involved in religious and social activities, advocating for peace and communal harmony in the region. Despite the controversies during his presidency, Zail Singh remained a respected figure, particularly among the Sikh community, for his deep religious conviction and his service to the nation.

Zail Singh passed away on December 25, 1994, following a car accident. His death was widely mourned, and he was remembered for his simplicity, humility, and dedication to public service. As a leader, Zail Singh's life reflected the complex interplay of religion, politics, and governance in a diverse and secular India.

Conclusion

GIANI ZAIL SINGH'S presidency was one of the most challenging in India's history, marked by significant political and communal turmoil. His deep-rooted faith, commitment to the principles of Sikhism, and loyalty to the Indian Constitution defined his tenure as President. While his term was marred by controversies, particularly during the 1984 anti-Sikh riots, Zail Singh's legacy as a leader who sought to balance his personal beliefs with his constitutional duties remains an important chapter in India's political history. His life and career serve as a reminder of the complexities and responsibilities that come with leadership in a diverse and democratic nation.

Chapter 8:
R. Venkataraman (1987–1992)

R. VENKATARAMAN SERVED as the eighth President of India from 1987 to 1992, a period marked by significant political changes and challenges. Known for his vast experience in public administration, finance, and law, Venkataraman brought a wealth of knowledge to the presidency. His tenure was characterized by his efforts to uphold constitutional integrity and navigate the complexities of coalition politics, economic challenges, and social unrest in a rapidly changing India.

Birth and Early Life

RAMASWAMY VENKATARAMAN was born on December 4, 1910, in Rajamadam, a village in the Tanjore district of the Madras Presidency (now Tamil Nadu). He came from a well-respected Brahmin family with deep roots in South Indian culture and traditions. His father, R. Narayanaswami, was a lawyer, and his upbringing was steeped in the values of education and public service.

Venkataraman's early life was shaped by the rich cultural and intellectual environment of Tamil Nadu. He was an excellent student, and his academic achievements laid the foundation for a future in law and politics. His formative years were also influenced by the growing nationalist movement in India, which ignited his passion for the country's independence.

Education and Early Career

VENKATARAMAN PURSUED his early education in Madras (now Chennai), where he attended the prestigious National College and later earned a law degree from the Law College, Madras. He quickly distinguished himself as a brilliant lawyer and began his legal practice in the Madras High Court in 1935. His legal acumen and dedication to justice earned him a reputation as a respected advocate.

However, the call of the independence movement was too strong to ignore. Venkataraman became actively involved in the Indian National Congress and the freedom struggle, inspired by leaders like Mahatma Gandhi and Jawaharlal Nehru. He participated in the Quit India Movement of 1942, which led to his imprisonment by the British authorities. His commitment to the cause of independence and his leadership within the Congress Party cemented his position as a rising star in Indian politics.

Political Career After Independence

AFTER INDIA'S INDEPENDENCE in 1947, R. Venkataraman continued his legal practice while also taking on significant roles in public administration. He was elected to the Constituent Assembly of India, where he contributed to the drafting of the Indian Constitution. His legal expertise was invaluable in shaping the framework of India's democracy.

Venkataraman's political career gained momentum in the 1950s when he was elected to the Lok Sabha, the lower house of Parliament. Over the years, he held several key positions in the Indian government, including Minister of Finance, Minister of Defence, and Minister of Home Affairs. His tenure as Finance Minister from 1980 to 1982 was particularly noteworthy, as he played a crucial role in managing India's economy during a period of global economic instability.

As Defence Minister from 1982 to 1984, Venkataraman oversaw important initiatives to modernize the Indian armed forces and strengthen the country's defense capabilities. His deep understanding of international relations and his efforts to build India's strategic partnerships were significant contributions to the nation's security.

Vice Presidency and Presidency

IN 1984, VENKATARAMAN was elected as the Vice President of India, a role that further prepared him for the presidency. His tenure as Vice President was marked by his efforts to maintain the dignity and neutrality of the office while supporting the smooth functioning of Parliament.

In 1987, R. Venkataraman was elected as the President of India, succeeding Giani Zail Singh. His presidency came at a time when India was grappling with several challenges, including economic difficulties, rising social unrest, and the complexities of coalition politics. Venkataraman's extensive experience in governance and his deep commitment to constitutional principles made him a stabilizing force during this period.

Major Contributions and Challenges

VENKATARAMAN'S PRESIDENCY was characterized by his efforts to uphold the Constitution and ensure the smooth functioning of the government. One of the most significant challenges he faced was the rise of coalition politics, which often led to political instability. During his tenure, India saw several changes in government, including the transition from the Rajiv Gandhi-led Congress government to the National Front government led by V.P. Singh in 1989.

As President, Venkataraman played a crucial role in managing these transitions, exercising his constitutional powers with caution and fairness. He maintained a non-partisan approach, respecting the democratic process while ensuring that the government remained stable and effective.

Venkataraman also faced the challenge of dealing with the growing social unrest in the country. The late 1980s and early 1990s were marked by increasing communal tensions, caste conflicts, and insurgencies in various parts of India. As President, he made numerous appeals for peace and unity, emphasizing the importance of maintaining communal harmony and upholding the rule of law.

During his tenure, India also witnessed the economic crisis of 1991, which led to significant changes in the country's economic policies. While Venkataraman's role as President was largely ceremonial, his support for the economic reforms introduced by the government of Prime Minister P.V. Narasimha Rao and Finance Minister Dr. Manmohan Singh was crucial in navigating the country through this difficult period.

Later Years and Legacy

AFTER COMPLETING HIS term as President in 1992, R. Venkataraman retired from active politics but continued to be an influential voice in public life. He remained committed to the values of democracy, social justice, and national unity, and he frequently spoke on issues of national importance.

Venkataraman's contributions to India were recognized through numerous awards and honors, both during his lifetime and posthumously. He passed away on January 27, 2009, at the age of 98, leaving behind a legacy of integrity, dedication, and service to the nation.

Conclusion

R. VENKATARAMAN'S LIFE and career exemplify the qualities of leadership, wisdom, and unwavering commitment to the nation. As the eighth President of India, he guided the country through a period of significant political and economic change, always adhering to the principles of the Constitution and the values of democracy. His legacy is one of service, integrity, and a deep respect for the institutions of Indian democracy. Venkataraman's contributions continue to inspire future generations of leaders, reminding us of the importance of experience, knowledge, and ethical governance in public life.

Chapter 9

Dr. Shankar Dayal Sharma (1992–1997)

DR. SHANKAR DAYAL SHARMA served as the ninth President of India from 1992 to 1997, a period that saw India undergoing significant political, economic, and social changes. Known for his scholarly demeanor, legal acumen, and deep commitment to democratic values, Dr. Sharma's presidency was marked by his efforts to maintain the dignity of the office and uphold the Constitution during a time of considerable challenges.

Birth and Early Life

SHANKAR DAYAL SHARMA was born on August 19, 1918, in Bhopal, which was then a princely state in British India. His family was well-known for its educational background and public service. His father, Dr. Khushilal Sharma, was a renowned Ayurvedic physician, which instilled in young Shankar Dayal a respect for learning and service to society.

From an early age, Sharma exhibited a keen intellect and a passion for academics. He completed his early education in Bhopal, excelling in his studies and earning scholarships that would take him to some of the most prestigious educational institutions in India and abroad.

Education and Early Career

SHANKAR DAYAL SHARMA'S academic journey was remarkable. He earned his Bachelor's degree from St. John's College, Agra, followed by a Master's degree in English Literature, History, and Political Science from the University of Lucknow. His pursuit of higher education led him to Fitzwilliam College, Cambridge, where he obtained a degree in Law, and later to Lincoln's Inn, London, where he became a barrister.

In addition to his legal studies, Sharma was also awarded a Ph.D. in Law from the University of Cambridge, a testament to his deep intellectual capabilities. His academic excellence earned him fellowships at prestigious institutions such as Harvard Law School. Sharma's education provided him with a strong foundation in constitutional law and public policy, which would later prove invaluable in his political career.

Political Career Before Presidency

DR. SHANKAR DAYAL SHARMA'S entry into politics was driven by his commitment to public service and the ideals of the Indian independence movement. He joined the Indian National Congress and became actively involved in the freedom struggle, participating in the Quit India Movement in 1942. His involvement in the independence movement led to his imprisonment by the British authorities, an experience that deepened his resolve to fight for India's freedom.

After India gained independence in 1947, Sharma continued his legal practice while also taking on leadership roles within the Congress Party. His political career took off in the early 1950s when he was elected as a member of the Madhya Pradesh Legislative Assembly. He quickly rose through the ranks, becoming the Chief Minister of Bhopal State from 1952 to 1956, and later holding important ministerial portfolios in Madhya Pradesh, including Education, Law, and Public Works.

Dr. Sharma's administrative skills and commitment to social justice earned him recognition at the national level. He served as the Union Minister for Communications from 1974 to 1977 and held various other key positions in the Indian government, including Governor of Andhra Pradesh, Punjab, and Maharashtra. His tenure as Governor was marked by his impartiality and strict adherence to constitutional principles, qualities that would define his later role as President.

Vice Presidency and Presidency

IN 1987, DR. SHANKAR Dayal Sharma was elected as the Vice President of India, a role that further solidified his reputation as a statesman and constitutional expert. As Vice President, he also served as the Chairman of the Rajya Sabha, where he was known for his fairness and commitment to democratic processes.

In 1992, Sharma was elected as the President of India, succeeding R. Venkataraman. His election was widely welcomed, given his vast experience in law, governance, and public administration. As President, Dr. Sharma's primary focus was on upholding the sanctity of the

Constitution and ensuring that the democratic institutions of the country functioned smoothly.

Major Contributions and Challenges

DR. SHARMA'S PRESIDENCY coincided with a period of significant change in India. The early 1990s saw the country grappling with economic liberalization, political instability, and social unrest. The demolition of the Babri Masjid in 1992 and the subsequent communal riots posed a serious challenge to the nation's secular fabric.

As President, Dr. Sharma was a strong advocate for maintaining communal harmony and upholding the rule of law. He made several appeals for peace and unity, urging political leaders and citizens alike to work together to preserve India's pluralistic society. His efforts to maintain calm during this tumultuous period were widely respected, although the communal tensions of the time remained a challenge for the country.

One of the most significant aspects of Dr. Sharma's presidency was his role in navigating the complexities of coalition politics. During his tenure, India saw multiple changes in government, with the rise of coalition politics leading to frequent shifts in power. Dr. Sharma's deep understanding of constitutional law was crucial in ensuring smooth transitions of power and maintaining the stability of the government.

His presidency also saw the beginning of India's economic liberalization under the leadership of Prime Minister P.V. Narasimha Rao and Finance Minister Dr. Manmohan Singh. Although the President's role in economic policy is limited, Dr. Sharma's support for the reforms was an important signal of stability and continuity at a time when India was opening up to global markets.

Later Years and Legacy

AFTER COMPLETING HIS term as President in 1997, Dr. Shankar Dayal Sharma retired from public life, although he continued to be an influential voice on matters of national importance. He remained committed to the ideals of democracy, secularism, and social justice, often speaking out on issues that he believed were critical to the nation's future.

Dr. Sharma passed away on December 26, 1999, at the age of 81. His death was widely mourned, and he was remembered as a scholar, statesman, and a man of deep principles. His legacy as President of India is marked by his unwavering commitment to the Constitution and his efforts to guide the nation through a period of significant change with wisdom and dignity.

Conclusion

DR. SHANKAR DAYAL SHARMA'S tenure as the ninth President of India was one of constitutional integrity, intellectual depth, and principled leadership. He guided the country through a challenging period with a steady hand, always prioritizing the values of democracy and social justice. His contributions to India, both as President and in his earlier roles, reflect a lifetime of service to the nation. Dr. Sharma's legacy continues to inspire future generations of leaders to uphold the principles of fairness, justice, and unity in the face of challenges.

K. R. Narayanan (1997–2002)

K. R. NARAYANAN SERVED as the tenth President of India from 1997 to 2002, and his tenure marked a series of firsts in the country's history. He was the first Dalit, or member of the historically marginalized communities in India, to occupy the highest constitutional office. Narayanan's presidency was characterized by his commitment to social justice, his defense of constitutional principles, and his role in navigating the complexities of Indian politics during a period of significant change.

Birth and Early Life

KOCHERIL RAMAN NARAYANAN was born on October 27, 1920, in the small village of Uzhavoor in the Kottayam district of Kerala. He was born into a humble family belonging to the Pulaya caste, a Dalit community, and faced the challenges of poverty and social discrimination from an early age. Despite these hardships, Narayanan's parents, Kocheril Raman Vaidyar and Punnaththuraveettil Paappiyamma, instilled in him the importance of education.

Narayanan's early life was marked by a thirst for knowledge and an insatiable curiosity. He attended local schools in Uzhavoor, where his academic brilliance quickly became apparent. His dedication to his studies earned him a scholarship to the University of Kerala, where he graduated with a Bachelor's degree in English literature in 1943. Narayanan's education provided him with a pathway out of poverty, but it also fueled his determination to fight against the social injustices that he and others from his community faced.

Education and Early Career

AFTER COMPLETING HIS education in Kerala, Narayanan moved to Delhi, where he studied at the prestigious Delhi School of Economics. However, his academic ambitions soon took him beyond India's borders. In 1945, Narayanan was awarded the Tata Scholarship to study at the London School of Economics (LSE), where he completed a degree in Political Science. At LSE, he was deeply influenced by the teachings of Harold Laski, a renowned political theorist, who further shaped Narayanan's views on democracy, governance, and social justice.

Upon returning to India, Narayanan began his career in journalism, working for newspapers like The Hindu and The Times of

India. However, his path soon shifted towards diplomacy. In 1949, at the recommendation of Prime Minister Jawaharlal Nehru, Narayanan joined the Indian Foreign Service (IFS), marking the beginning of a distinguished career in international diplomacy.

Diplomatic Career

AS A DIPLOMAT, K. R. Narayanan served in various capacities in several countries, including Burma (now Myanmar), Japan, the United Kingdom, Turkey, and China. His diplomatic skills were widely recognized, and he played a crucial role in representing India's interests abroad during the early years of its independence.

One of Narayanan's most significant contributions came during his tenure as India's Ambassador to the United States from 1980 to 1984. This period was marked by Cold War tensions, and Narayanan's diplomatic acumen helped to strengthen Indo-US relations, particularly in the areas of trade and defense. His efforts earned him respect both in India and abroad, solidifying his reputation as a capable and principled diplomat.

Entry into Politics

NARAYANAN'S SUCCESSFUL diplomatic career set the stage for his entry into Indian politics. In 1984, he was invited by Prime Minister Indira Gandhi to join the Indian National Congress (INC) and contest the Lok Sabha elections. Narayanan won a seat from the Ottapalam constituency in Kerala and quickly established himself as a knowledgeable and articulate parliamentarian.

During his time in Parliament, Narayanan served as Minister of State for Planning, External Affairs, and later Science and Technology. His contributions to these ministries were significant, particularly in the areas of international relations, economic planning, and technological advancement. His political career was marked by a deep commitment to the welfare of marginalized communities and a firm belief in the importance of social justice in India's development.

Vice Presidency and Presidency

IN 1992, K. R. NARAYANAN was elected as the Vice President of India, a role that further prepared him for the presidency. As Vice President, he also served as the Chairman of the Rajya Sabha, where he was known for his fairness and impartiality in conducting the proceedings of the upper house.

In 1997, Narayanan was elected as the President of India, succeeding Dr. Shankar Dayal Sharma. His election was historic, as he became the first Dalit to hold the office of President, symbolizing a significant step forward for social inclusion and representation in India.

Major Contributions and Challenges

NARAYANAN'S PRESIDENCY was characterized by his deep commitment to upholding the Constitution and his willingness to speak out on issues of national importance. One of the most notable aspects of his tenure was his decision to depart from the traditional, largely ceremonial role of the President and take a more active stance on matters of governance.

During his presidency, Narayanan faced several political challenges, including the fall of the I. K. Gujral government in 1997 and the subsequent political instability. He played a crucial role in ensuring that the transitions of power were conducted smoothly and in accordance with the Constitution. Narayanan's insistence on following due process was evident in 1998, when he called for a vote of confidence in Parliament before inviting Atal Bihari Vajpayee to form the government.

Narayanan was also a vocal advocate for social justice and equality. He used his position to highlight the issues faced by marginalized communities, particularly Dalits and Adivasis, and frequently called for greater efforts to address social and economic disparities in the country. His speeches and public statements often reflected his belief in the principles of social justice, secularism, and democracy.

One of the most challenging moments of his presidency came in 2002, during the Gujarat riots. Narayanan expressed his deep concern over the communal violence and urged the government to take swift action to restore peace and protect the rights of all citizens. His stance during this period earned him both praise and criticism, but it underscored his commitment to the values enshrined in the Indian Constitution.

Later Years and Legacy

AFTER COMPLETING HIS term as President in 2002, K. R. Narayanan retired from public life. He remained a respected figure in Indian society, known for his integrity, intellect, and unwavering commitment to social justice. Narayanan passed away on November 9, 2005, at the age of 85. His death was widely mourned, and he was remembered as a trailblazer who broke barriers and set new standards for the office of the President.

Conclusion

K. R. NARAYANAN'S PRESIDENCY was a defining period in Indian history, marked by his efforts to uphold constitutional values, promote social justice, and navigate the complexities of a changing nation. His life and career stand as a testament to the power of education, perseverance, and principled leadership in overcoming adversity. As the first Dalit President of India, Narayanan's legacy is one of empowerment and inclusion, inspiring future generations to strive for a more just and equitable society. His contributions to Indian politics, diplomacy, and social reform continue to resonate, making him one of the most respected and admired leaders in the country's history.

Chapter 11:
Dr. A. P. J. Abdul Kalam (2002–2007)

DR. A. P. J. ABDUL Kalam, often referred to as the "Missile Man of India," served as the 11th President of India from 2002 to 2007. His tenure as President was marked by his dedication to science, education, and the development of India, as well as his deep connection with the youth of the country. Kalam's presidency was unique, as he was a scientist and engineer first, and a politician second, which brought a fresh perspective to the highest office in the land.

Birth and Early Life

AVUL PAKIR JAINULABDEEN Abdul Kalam was born on October 15, 1931, in the small town of Rameswaram in Tamil Nadu. His family was of modest means; his father, Jainulabdeen, was a boat owner and imam of a local mosque, while his mother, Ashiamma, was a homemaker. Despite their limited resources, Kalam's parents placed great emphasis on education and spirituality, values that deeply influenced him throughout his life.

Kalam's early life was not easy. He had to work to support his family, distributing newspapers after school to contribute to the household income. However, his passion for learning never waned. He was a diligent student with a particular interest in mathematics and science, subjects that would later become the cornerstone of his illustrious career.

Education and Early Career

KALAM COMPLETED HIS schooling at the Schwartz Higher Secondary School in Ramanathapuram. His academic excellence earned him a scholarship to attend St. Joseph's College in Tiruchirappalli, where he graduated with a degree in Physics in 1954. However, his true calling was in engineering, which led him to pursue a degree in Aerospace Engineering from the Madras Institute of Technology (MIT).

At MIT, Kalam's passion for aeronautics blossomed. He was known for his dedication and innovative thinking, qualities that caught the attention of his professors and peers. After graduating in 1960, Kalam joined the Aeronautical Development Establishment of the Defence Research and Development Organisation (DRDO) as a scientist. This marked the beginning of a remarkable career in India's defense and space research sectors.

Scientific Achievements

KALAM'S CONTRIBUTIONS to India's defense capabilities are legendary. In the early 1960s, he joined the Indian Space Research Organisation (ISRO) where he played a pivotal role in the development of India's first indigenous Satellite Launch Vehicle (SLV-III), which successfully deployed the Rohini satellite into orbit in 1980. This achievement marked India's entry into the space club and laid the foundation for future advancements in space exploration.

Kalam's work in missile technology was equally groundbreaking. He returned to DRDO in the 1980s to lead the Integrated Guided Missile Development Programme (IGMDP), which resulted in the successful development of the Agni and Prithvi missiles. These projects earned him the nickname "Missile Man" and significantly enhanced India's defense capabilities.

His contributions were recognized with numerous awards, including the Padma Bhushan in 1981, the Padma Vibhushan in 1990, and the Bharat Ratna, India's highest civilian honor, in 1997. Beyond his technical achievements, Kalam was known for his visionary ideas about India's future, particularly his dream of transforming India into a developed nation by 2020, outlined in his book *India 2020: A Vision for the New Millennium*.

Presidency

IN 2002, A. P. J. ABDUL Kalam was elected as the President of India, with the support of both the ruling National Democratic Alliance (NDA) and the opposition parties. His election was unique as he was a scientist and a technocrat with no political background, yet his popularity transcended political boundaries, making him a unifying figure.

As President, Kalam brought his characteristic humility, simplicity, and forward-thinking vision to the Rashtrapati Bhavan. He was deeply committed to the idea of India as a developed, self-reliant nation and emphasized the importance of science and technology in achieving this goal. Throughout his presidency, Kalam continued to engage with young people, often referred to as the "People's President" due to his accessibility and connection with the masses.

One of the most notable aspects of Kalam's presidency was his focus on education and youth empowerment. He believed that India's future depended on the creativity and innovation of its younger generation, and he made it a point to interact with students across the country. His inspirational speeches and writings motivated millions of young Indians to dream big and contribute to the nation's progress.

During his tenure, Kalam also dealt with significant political challenges, including the contentious Office of Profit Bill and the Gujarat riots of 2002. Despite these challenges, he maintained the dignity of the presidential office and upheld the Constitution with impartiality.

Major Contributions and Legacy

DR. A. P. J. ABDUL Kalam's presidency was marked by his commitment to national development, science, and education. He initiated several programs aimed at promoting scientific research and innovation in India, including the PURA (Providing Urban Amenities in Rural Areas) scheme, which aimed to bridge the urban-rural divide.

Kalam's vision for India was not limited to technological advancements; he also emphasized the importance of moral leadership and ethical governance. He often spoke about the need for integrity and transparency in public life and encouraged leaders to serve the nation with dedication and honesty.

After his presidency ended in 2007, Kalam returned to what he loved most—teaching and inspiring the youth. He became a visiting professor at several universities and continued to engage with students across the country. His books, including *Wings of Fire*, *Ignited

Minds*, and *My Journey: Transforming Dreams into Actions*, continue to inspire millions.

Later Years and Passing

EVEN AFTER HIS TENURE as President, Kalam remained a beloved figure in India. He was active in public life, giving lectures, writing books, and interacting with students. His dedication to education and his vision for India's future never wavered.

On July 27, 2015, while delivering a lecture at the Indian Institute of Management Shillong, Dr. A. P. J. Abdul Kalam collapsed and passed away from a cardiac arrest. His sudden death shocked the nation, and tributes poured in from all corners of the world. His funeral was attended by thousands, including dignitaries, students, and ordinary citizens who were touched by his life and work.

Conclusion

DR. A. P. J. ABDUL Kalam's life was a remarkable journey from humble beginnings to the highest office in India. His contributions to science, defense, and education left an indelible mark on the nation. As President, he brought a unique blend of intellect, vision, and humility to the role, inspiring millions of Indians to dream big and work towards a brighter future. Kalam's legacy as the "People's President" and a visionary leader continues to inspire and guide India towards the path of progress and development.

PRATIBHA PATIL SERVED as the 12th President of India from 2007 to 2012, making history as the first woman to hold the office. Her presidency was marked by her focus on issues related to women's empowerment, education, and social welfare. Patil's election to the highest constitutional office in India was a significant milestone, reflecting the progress of women in Indian society and politics.

Birth and Early Life

PRATIBHA DEVISINGH Patil was born on December 19, 1934, in the small town of Nadgaon in the Jalgaon district of Maharashtra. She was born into a simple, middle-class family. Her father, Narayan Rao Patil, was a government clerk, and her mother, Shakuntala, was a homemaker. From an early age, Patil displayed a strong sense of discipline, responsibility, and a deep commitment to education, qualities that would later define her public life.

Growing up in a conservative society where opportunities for women were limited, Patil's father ensured she received a good education. She completed her early schooling in Jalgaon and went on to pursue higher studies at Mooljee Jaitha College, where she earned her bachelor's degree in Arts. Patil then attended Government Law College in Mumbai, where she completed her law degree, becoming one of the few women in her region to do so at the time.

Entry into Politics

PATIL'S ENTRY INTO politics was influenced by her family's involvement in the Indian freedom movement and her own desire to contribute to public service. She began her political career in 1962 when she was elected as a member of the Maharashtra Legislative Assembly from the Edlabad constituency. At the young age of 27, Patil's election marked the beginning of a long and distinguished career in public service.

During her time in the Maharashtra Legislative Assembly, Patil quickly made a name for herself as a diligent and effective legislator. She held various important portfolios in the Maharashtra government, including the ministries of Public Health, Social Welfare, Housing, and Education. Patil's work in these areas was widely recognized, particularly her efforts to improve healthcare and education for women and children in the state.

Her commitment to social welfare extended beyond her legislative duties. Patil was actively involved in various social causes, particularly those related to women's rights and empowerment. She was instrumental in the establishment of several institutions that aimed to provide education and vocational training to women, helping them achieve financial independence and social equality.

National Politics and Governorship

PATIL'S SUCCESS IN state politics led to her entry into national politics. In 1985, she was elected to the Rajya Sabha, the upper house of India's Parliament. During her tenure in the Rajya Sabha, Patil continued her advocacy for social justice, focusing on issues related to gender equality, education, and public health.

In 1991, Patil was elected to the Lok Sabha, representing the Amravati constituency in Maharashtra. Her work as a parliamentarian was marked by her dedication to her constituents and her efforts to bring about legislative reforms that benefited the underprivileged and marginalized sections of society.

In 2004, Patil was appointed as the Governor of Rajasthan, becoming the first woman to hold this position in the state. Her tenure as Governor was marked by her focus on improving the status of women in Rajasthan, a state known for its deeply rooted patriarchal traditions. Patil worked to promote education for girls, improve healthcare facilities, and support initiatives aimed at empowering women economically.

Presidency

IN 2007, PRATIBHA PATIL was nominated as the United Progressive Alliance (UPA) candidate for the presidency. Her nomination was historic, as she was the first woman to be nominated for the office of President of India. Despite facing some controversy and opposition, Patil was elected as the 12th President of India on July 25, 2007, with a substantial majority.

Patil's presidency was marked by her focus on issues related to women's empowerment, education, and social welfare. She used her position to advocate for greater representation of women in all spheres of life, from politics and business to education and healthcare. Patil also emphasized the importance of education as a means of social and economic upliftment, particularly for women and disadvantaged communities.

During her tenure, Patil traveled extensively within India and abroad, representing the country on various international platforms. She played a significant role in strengthening India's diplomatic relations with other nations, promoting peace, cooperation, and mutual understanding.

Patil's presidency was also characterized by her efforts to maintain the dignity and integrity of the office. She upheld the constitutional values of India and worked to ensure that the presidency remained above the fray of partisan politics. Her leadership was seen as calm, steady, and focused on the welfare of the people.

Major Contributions and Challenges

ONE OF PATIL'S SIGNIFICANT contributions as President was her emphasis on the importance of social justice and inclusive development. She often spoke about the need for policies and programs that addressed the needs of the most vulnerable sections of society, including women, children, and the elderly.

Patil also focused on the importance of education in nation-building. She believed that education was the key to unlocking India's potential and worked to promote initiatives that aimed at increasing literacy rates, particularly among women and girls. Her advocacy for education was not just limited to formal schooling; she also supported vocational training programs that provided skills and employment opportunities to those in need.

During her presidency, Patil faced several challenges, including the global economic crisis of 2008, which had a significant impact on India's economy. Despite these challenges, she remained focused on her mission to promote social welfare and economic development.

Later Years and Legacy

AFTER COMPLETING HER term as President in 2012, Pratibha Patil retired from public life. She returned to her home state of Maharashtra, where she continued to be involved in social work and remained a respected figure in Indian society.

Patil's legacy as the first woman President of India is significant. Her election to the highest constitutional office in the country was a symbol of the progress women had made in Indian society and politics. Throughout her career, Patil remained committed to the causes of women's empowerment, education, and social justice, leaving behind a legacy of compassion, dedication, and service to the nation.

Conclusion

PRATIBHA PATIL'S PRESIDENCY marked a historic chapter in India's history, as she broke new ground as the country's first woman President. Her life and career are a testament to the power of perseverance, education, and dedication to public service. Patil's work in promoting women's rights, education, and social welfare continues to inspire future generations. As President, she upheld the values of the Indian Constitution, maintaining the dignity of the office and working towards a more inclusive and equitable society. Her contributions to Indian politics and society will be remembered as a significant milestone in the country's journey towards gender equality and social justice.

Chapter 13

Pranab Mukherjee (2012–2017)

PRANAB MUKHERJEE, OFTEN referred to as the "Congressman for all seasons," served as the 13th President of India from 2012 to 2017. His presidency marked the culmination of a long and illustrious political career that spanned over five decades. Mukherjee's deep understanding of the Indian political landscape, coupled with his vast experience in various key government roles, made him one of the most respected and influential statesmen in India.

Birth and Early Life

PRANAB KUMAR MUKHERJEE was born on December 11, 1935, in the small village of Mirati in the Birbhum district of West Bengal. He was born into a family with a strong political background; his father, Kamada Kinkar Mukherjee, was a freedom fighter and a member of the Indian National Congress, who spent significant time in British prisons for his role in the independence movement. His mother, Rajlakshmi Mukherjee, was a homemaker.

Growing up in a politically active family, Mukherjee was exposed to the ideas of nationalism and public service from an early age. He completed his schooling at the Suri Vidyasagar College in Birbhum, and later earned a master's degree in Political Science and History as well as a degree in Law from the University of Calcutta. His academic background laid the foundation for his deep understanding of political theory and law, which would serve him well in his future political career.

Early Career and Entry into Politics

BEFORE ENTERING POLITICS, Mukherjee worked as a college teacher and a journalist. He began his professional career as a lecturer in Political Science at the Vidyanagar College in Kolkata, and later worked for the Desher Dak, a Bengali-language newspaper. However, it was his entry into politics that truly defined his career.

Mukherjee's political journey began in the early 1960s when he joined the Indian National Congress, following in his father's footsteps. His political acumen and dedication quickly caught the attention of senior Congress leaders, including then-Prime Minister Indira Gandhi. In 1969, Mukherjee was elected to the Rajya Sabha, the upper house of the Indian Parliament, marking the beginning of his long and distinguished political career.

Political Rise and Key Government Roles

PRANAB MUKHERJEE'S rise in Indian politics was rapid. He became a key figure in the Indian National Congress and was known for his ability to navigate complex political situations with ease. Over the years, Mukherjee held several important positions in the Indian government, showcasing his versatility and expertise in various domains.

One of his earliest major roles was as the Union Minister of Commerce and Industry in 1980, where he played a crucial role in shaping India's trade policies. In 1982, he was appointed as the Union Minister of Finance, a position that solidified his reputation as an able administrator and policymaker. During his tenure as Finance Minister, Mukherjee was credited with steering India through a challenging economic period and laying the groundwork for future economic reforms.

Mukherjee also served as the Minister of External Affairs twice, first from 1995 to 1996 and again from 2006 to 2009. His diplomatic skills were evident in his handling of India's foreign relations, particularly during a time of significant global changes. He was instrumental in improving India's relations with its neighbors and major global powers, ensuring that India's voice was heard on the international stage.

In addition to these roles, Mukherjee also served as the Minister of Defence from 2004 to 2006, where he oversaw key defense initiatives and played a pivotal role in modernizing India's armed forces. His experience and knowledge across various ministries made him a trusted advisor to multiple Prime Ministers, and he was often regarded as the "troubleshooter" of the Congress party.

Presidency

IN 2012, PRANAB MUKHERJEE was elected as the 13th President of India. His election was seen as a recognition of his decades of service to the nation and his deep understanding of the workings of the Indian government. Mukherjee's presidency was marked by his adherence to constitutional principles, his respect for parliamentary democracy, and his efforts to uphold the dignity of the office.

As President, Mukherjee brought his vast experience and knowledge to the Rashtrapati Bhavan. He was known for his meticulous attention to detail and his ability to balance the various roles of the presidency—being a ceremonial head of state, a constitutional guardian, and a moral authority. Mukherjee was particularly mindful of maintaining the independence of the presidency, ensuring that the office remained above partisan politics.

During his tenure, Mukherjee dealt with several significant political and constitutional issues. He played a crucial role in managing the delicate balance of power between the executive, the legislature, and the judiciary. Mukherjee's decisions, particularly those related to the use of presidential powers such as granting pardons and returning bills for reconsideration, were guided by his deep respect for the Constitution and democratic principles.

Mukherjee was also a strong advocate for education and innovation. He frequently interacted with students and young leaders, encouraging them to take an active role in nation-building. He also launched several initiatives to promote innovation and research, believing that education was key to India's progress.

Major Contributions and Legacy

PRANAB MUKHERJEE'S contributions to Indian politics and governance are vast and varied. As a statesman, he was instrumental in shaping India's economic, defense, and foreign policies over several decades. His leadership during critical moments, such as the economic crisis of the early 1980s and the Kargil War in 1999, demonstrated his ability to handle complex challenges with wisdom and foresight.

Mukherjee's tenure as President was marked by his commitment to upholding the values of the Indian Constitution. He often spoke about the importance of tolerance, pluralism, and the need for dialogue in a diverse democracy like India. His speeches and writings emphasized the need for ethical governance, transparency, and accountability in public life.

Mukherjee's legacy as a statesman and a scholar is reflected in the numerous awards and honors he received during his lifetime, including the Bharat Ratna, India's highest civilian award, which was conferred upon him in 2019. His autobiography, *The Presidential Years*, provides insights into his thoughts on governance, politics, and the challenges of leading a diverse and complex nation like India.

Later Years and Passing

AFTER COMPLETING HIS term as President in 2017, Pranab Mukherjee continued to be an influential voice in Indian public life. He remained engaged in discussions on national issues and was often called upon to share his wisdom and experience.

However, his health began to decline in his later years. In August 2020, Mukherjee was hospitalized after testing positive for COVID-19 and undergoing surgery for a brain clot. Despite the best efforts of medical professionals, he passed away on August 31, 2020, at the age of 84. His death was mourned across the nation, with leaders from all political parties paying tribute to his legacy and contributions to India.

Conclusion

PRANAB MUKHERJEE'S life was a testament to dedication, perseverance, and a deep commitment to public service. His journey from a small village in West Bengal to the highest office in India is an inspiring story of how knowledge, hard work, and integrity can shape a nation's destiny. As President, Mukherjee upheld the dignity and sanctity of the office, and his legacy as a statesman, scholar, and leader continues to inspire future generations. His contributions to India's political and economic landscape, as well as his commitment to constitutional values, have left an indelible mark on the nation's history.

RAM NATH KOVIND SERVED as the 14th President of India from 2017 to 2022. His tenure was marked by his dedication to upholding the values of the Indian Constitution and his commitment to the welfare of marginalized communities. Coming from a humble background, Kovind's rise to the highest constitutional office in the country is a testament to his perseverance, integrity, and unwavering belief in democratic principles.

Birth and Early Life

RAM NATH KOVIND WAS born on October 1, 1945, in the small village of Paraunkh in the Kanpur Dehat district of Uttar Pradesh. He was born into a Dalit family, and his early life was shaped by the challenges of growing up in a socially and economically disadvantaged community. His father, Maiku Lal Kovind, was a farmer and a local Vaidya (traditional medicine practitioner), while his mother, Kalawati, was a homemaker. Kovind was the youngest of five siblings.

Despite the economic hardships, Kovind was determined to pursue his education. He attended a local primary school in his village and later moved to Kanpur for higher studies. Kovind graduated with a degree in commerce from DAV College in Kanpur and subsequently earned a degree in law from DAV College's affiliated Kanpur University (now Chhatrapati Shahu Ji Maharaj University). His academic achievements were a source of pride for his family and community, and they laid the foundation for his future career.

Early Career and Legal Practice

AFTER COMPLETING HIS law degree, Kovind moved to Delhi to prepare for the civil services examination. Although he passed the prestigious exam, he opted out of joining the services and instead chose to practice law. Kovind enrolled as an advocate with the bar council in 1971 and began practicing law in the Delhi High Court and the Supreme Court of India.

Kovind's legal career was marked by his commitment to social justice and his advocacy for the rights of the underprivileged. He served as the Central Government's advocate in the Delhi High Court from 1977 to 1979 and later as the Central Government's standing counsel in the Supreme Court from 1980 to 1993. His legal practice brought him into contact with a wide range of issues, including civil rights, social justice, and constitutional law, which deepened his understanding of the legal and social challenges facing the country.

Political Career

RAM NATH KOVIND'S ENTRY into politics was driven by his desire to work for the upliftment of marginalized communities, particularly Dalits. He joined the Bharatiya Janata Party (BJP) in 1991 and quickly became an active member of the party. Kovind's political career was closely aligned with his commitment to social justice, and he became known for his efforts to improve the lives of Dalits and other disadvantaged groups.

In 1994, Kovind was elected to the Rajya Sabha, representing the state of Uttar Pradesh. He served as a member of the upper house for 12 years, during which time he played an important role in shaping policies related to social justice, education, and rural development. Kovind was also a member of several parliamentary committees, including the Committee on Welfare of Scheduled Castes and Scheduled Tribes, the Parliamentary Committee on Social Justice and Empowerment, and the Parliamentary Committee on Law and Justice.

During his tenure in the Rajya Sabha, Kovind was recognized for his dedication to the welfare of marginalized communities and his efforts to promote education and economic opportunities for them. He also represented India at the United Nations and addressed the UN General Assembly in 2002, highlighting India's commitment to democracy and social justice.

Governor of Bihar

IN 2015, KOVIND WAS appointed as the Governor of Bihar, a position he held until 2017. His tenure as governor was marked by his impartiality, integrity, and focus on good governance. Kovind worked closely with the state government to improve the delivery of public services and promote development in the state, particularly in rural and backward areas.

As governor, Kovind was known for his efforts to promote education, especially for girls and disadvantaged communities. He was also instrumental in ensuring that the benefits of government schemes reached the people who needed them the most. Kovind's tenure as governor earned him the respect and admiration of people across the political spectrum, and he was widely regarded as a model of how a constitutional office should be conducted.

Presidency

IN 2017, RAM NATH KOVIND was nominated as the presidential candidate by the ruling National Democratic Alliance (NDA). His candidacy was supported by several political parties, including those outside the NDA, reflecting his broad appeal and the respect he commanded across party lines. Kovind was elected as the 14th President of India on July 25, 2017, becoming the second Dalit to hold the office after K. R. Narayanan.

Kovind's presidency was marked by his commitment to upholding the values enshrined in the Indian Constitution. He emphasized the importance of inclusivity, social justice, and the rule of law in his speeches and actions. Kovind frequently spoke about the need to bridge the gap between different sections of society and to work towards creating a more equitable and just nation.

During his tenure, Kovind handled several significant constitutional and political challenges with wisdom and tact. He was known for his calm and measured approach to complex issues and his ability to rise above partisan politics. Kovind also focused on the welfare of the armed forces and veterans, often highlighting their sacrifices and contributions to the nation.

Kovind's presidency was also characterized by his efforts to connect with ordinary citizens. He traveled extensively across the country, visiting remote areas and interacting with people from diverse backgrounds. Kovind's humility and approachability endeared him to many, and he was widely regarded as a "people's president."

Major Contributions and Legacy

RAM NATH KOVIND'S CONTRIBUTIONS to Indian society and politics are rooted in his lifelong commitment to social justice and the welfare of marginalized communities. As President, he used his position to advocate for the rights of Dalits, women, and other disadvantaged groups. He emphasized the importance of education, particularly for girls and children from marginalized communities, as a means of empowering them and enabling them to contribute to the nation's development.

Kovind's tenure as President was marked by his efforts to uphold the dignity and sanctity of the office. He was known for his adherence to constitutional principles and his respect for the democratic process. Kovind's leadership was characterized by his humility, integrity, and dedication to the welfare of the people.

One of Kovind's most significant contributions was his focus on promoting social harmony and national unity. He often spoke about the need for mutual respect and understanding between different communities and stressed the importance of India's diversity as a source of strength. Kovind's presidency was a reminder of the importance of inclusivity and social justice in building a strong and united nation.

Later Years and Retirement

AFTER COMPLETING HIS term as President in 2022, Ram Nath Kovind retired from public life. He returned to his home in Uttar Pradesh, where he continued to engage in social work and remained a respected figure in Indian society. Kovind's legacy as a leader who rose from humble beginnings to become the President of India serves as an inspiration to millions of people, particularly those from marginalized communities.

Kovind's life and career are a testament to the power of education, perseverance, and a commitment to public service. His contributions to Indian society and politics, particularly in the areas of social justice and the welfare of marginalized communities, have left an indelible mark on the nation's history.

Conclusion

RAM NATH KOVIND'S PRESIDENCY was a significant chapter in India's democratic journey. As the 14th President of India, he upheld the values of the Constitution and worked tirelessly for the welfare of the people, particularly those from marginalized communities. Kovind's leadership, humility, and dedication to social justice have left a lasting legacy, and his life story continues to inspire future generations to strive for a more inclusive and equitable society.

Chapter 15:
Droupadi Murmu (2022–Present)

DROUPADI MURMU'S RISE to the position of the 15th President of India in 2022 marked a historic moment for the nation. As the first tribal woman and the second woman overall to hold the office, her presidency represents a significant milestone in India's journey toward inclusivity and representation. Murmu's life story is one of resilience, determination, and dedication to public service, and her tenure as President is seen as a symbol of hope for marginalized communities across the country.

Birth and Early Life

DROUPADI MURMU WAS born on June 20, 1958, in the small tribal village of Uparbeda in the Mayurbhanj district of Odisha. She belongs to the Santhal community, one of the largest tribal groups in India. Her father, Biranchi Narayan Tudu, and her grandfather were village heads, and Murmu grew up in a family that was deeply rooted in the traditions and culture of their community.

Growing up in a remote and underdeveloped region, Murmu faced significant challenges, including limited access to education and basic amenities. Despite these obstacles, she was determined to pursue her studies. Murmu attended a local school in her village before moving to Bhubaneswar, where she completed her higher education. She earned a Bachelor of Arts degree from Rama Devi Women's College in Bhubaneswar, becoming one of the few women from her community to achieve higher education.

Early Career

BEFORE ENTERING POLITICS, Droupadi Murmu worked as a teacher and later as a clerk in the Odisha government's irrigation department. Her early career was marked by her commitment to education and social welfare, and she was known for her dedication to improving the lives of those around her. Murmu's work as a teacher allowed her to connect with young people in her community and inspire them to pursue their dreams, despite the challenges they faced.

Political Career

MURMU'S ENTRY INTO politics was driven by her desire to serve her community and work for the upliftment of marginalized groups. She joined the Bharatiya Janata Party (BJP) in the late 1990s and quickly rose through the ranks, becoming an active member of the party in Odisha. Her political career began in earnest when she was elected as a councilor in the Rairangpur Nagar Panchayat in 1997. She served as the Vice-Chairperson of the Panchayat and gained a reputation for her hard work and dedication to public service.

In 2000, Murmu was elected as a Member of the Legislative Assembly (MLA) from the Rairangpur constituency in Odisha. She served two consecutive terms as an MLA and was a minister in the Odisha government, holding portfolios such as Commerce, Transport, Fisheries, and Animal Husbandry. As a minister, Murmu focused on issues related to rural development, agriculture, and tribal welfare, areas that were close to her heart given her background.

Murmu's political career was marked by her commitment to addressing the needs of tribal communities and other marginalized groups. She was known for her grassroots approach to politics, often traveling to remote areas to listen to the concerns of the people and advocate for their rights. Her work in Odisha earned her widespread respect and recognition, both within her party and among the general public.

Governor of Jharkhand

IN 2015, DROUPADI MURMU was appointed as the Governor of Jharkhand, becoming the first woman and the first tribal leader to hold the position. Her tenure as governor was marked by her efforts to promote tribal welfare and development in the state. Jharkhand, with its significant tribal population, presented both challenges and opportunities for Murmu, and she approached her role with the same dedication and commitment that had characterized her political career.

As governor, Murmu focused on improving education, healthcare, and infrastructure in tribal areas. She also worked to protect the rights of tribal communities, particularly in matters related to land ownership and resource management. Murmu's tenure was noted for her ability to balance the interests of the state government with the needs of the tribal population, ensuring that development efforts were inclusive and respectful of local traditions and customs.

Murmu's time as governor was also marked by her efforts to promote social harmony and communal peace. She was a strong advocate for dialogue and understanding between different communities and worked to address issues of conflict and division in the state. Her leadership in Jharkhand further solidified her reputation as a dedicated public servant and a champion of marginalized communities.

Presidency

DROUPADI MURMU'S ELECTION as the 15th President of India in July 2022 was a moment of immense pride for the nation, particularly for tribal communities. Her candidacy, supported by the ruling National Democratic Alliance (NDA), was seen as a recognition of the contributions of tribal communities to India's development and a step toward greater inclusivity in the country's leadership.

Murmu's presidency is significant not only for her personal achievements but also for what it represents in the broader context of India's democratic journey. As the first tribal woman to hold the office, Murmu's election symbolizes the progress India has made in ensuring that all sections of society have a voice in the country's governance. Her presidency is a source of inspiration for millions of people, particularly women and members of marginalized communities, who see in her a reflection of their own aspirations and dreams.

Since taking office, President Murmu has emphasized the importance of unity, social justice, and inclusive development in her speeches and public engagements. She has called for greater efforts to address the needs of marginalized communities, particularly in areas such as education, healthcare, and economic empowerment. Murmu's presidency is also marked by her focus on environmental sustainability and the protection of natural resources, particularly in regions inhabited by tribal communities. Recognizing the deep connection that many indigenous communities have with their natural environment, she has advocated for policies that promote sustainable development while respecting the rights and traditions of these communities.

Murmu has also been a vocal advocate for women's empowerment, emphasizing the need for greater gender equality in all spheres of life. In her speeches, she has highlighted the importance of education for girls and the need to create more opportunities for women to participate in the workforce and in leadership roles. Her own journey from a small tribal village to the highest office in the country serves as a powerful example of what women can achieve when they are given the opportunity to realize their potential.

Another significant aspect of Murmu's presidency is her commitment to social harmony and national unity. She has consistently called for bridging the divides between different communities, whether based on religion, caste, or ethnicity. In a country as diverse as India, Murmu's message of unity and inclusion resonates strongly, and she has used her platform as President to promote mutual respect and understanding among all citizens.

Murmu has also placed a strong emphasis on the importance of democratic values and the rule of law. She has spoken about the need to strengthen democratic institutions and ensure that the principles of justice, liberty, and equality are upheld. In her role as the guardian of the Constitution, Murmu has been steadfast in her commitment to protecting the rights of all citizens, particularly those who are most vulnerable.

As the country's first tribal President, Murmu has brought attention to the unique challenges faced by tribal communities across India. She has advocated for greater investment in education, healthcare, and infrastructure in tribal areas, and has called for more inclusive policies that address the specific needs of these communities.

Murmu's presidency has thus helped to bring issues related to tribal welfare to the forefront of national discourse.

Murmu's approach to the presidency has been characterized by her humility and accessibility. Despite holding the highest office in the country, she remains deeply connected to her roots and continues to engage with people from all walks of life. Whether meeting with world leaders or visiting remote villages, Murmu has consistently emphasized the importance of listening to the voices of ordinary citizens and working to address their concerns.

Legacy and Impact

ALTHOUGH DROUPADI MURMU'S presidency is still ongoing, her impact is already being felt across India. Her election has been a source of pride and inspiration for tribal communities, women, and other marginalized groups, who see in her a powerful symbol of what is possible in a democratic society. Murmu's focus on social justice, environmental sustainability, and national unity has resonated with people from all backgrounds, and she has quickly become a respected and admired figure in Indian public life.

Murmu's presidency also represents a significant step forward in India's journey toward greater inclusivity and representation. Her election has demonstrated that the highest office in the land is accessible to all citizens, regardless of their background, and has underscored the importance of diversity in leadership. As India continues to evolve and grow as a nation, Murmu's presidency serves as a reminder of the strength that comes from embracing the country's rich diversity.

Conclusion

DROUPADI MURMU'S TENURE as the 15th President of India is a historic milestone in the country's democratic journey. Her life story, marked by perseverance, dedication, and a commitment to public service, is an inspiration to millions. As the first tribal woman to hold the office of President, Murmu's legacy will be defined by her efforts to promote inclusivity, social justice, and national unity. Her presidency is not just a personal achievement, but a testament to the progress India has made in ensuring that its leadership reflects the diverse voices and aspirations of its people.

Part II
Prime Ministers of India

Chapter 1:
Jawaharlal Nehru (1947–1964)

JAWAHARLAL NEHRU, INDIA'S first Prime Minister, served from 1947 to 1964, guiding the nation through its formative years after independence. Nehru's leadership, vision, and policies played a pivotal role in shaping modern India, laying the foundations for democracy, secularism, and economic development. His tenure as Prime Minister remains one of the most significant periods in Indian history, characterized by his commitment to building a strong, united, and progressive nation.

Birth and Early Life

JAWAHARLAL NEHRU WAS born on November 14, 1889, in Allahabad (now Prayagraj), in British India. He was born into a wealthy and influential family; his father, Motilal Nehru, was a prominent lawyer and an active figure in the Indian National Congress. Nehru's mother, Swaruprani Thussu, came from a well-known Kashmiri Brahmin family. Growing up in a privileged environment, Nehru received an excellent education, both in India and abroad.

Nehru's early education took place at home under the supervision of private tutors. In 1905, he was sent to Harrow, an elite boarding school in England, and later attended Trinity College, Cambridge, where he earned a degree in natural sciences. Following his graduation, Nehru studied law at the Inner Temple in London and qualified as a barrister. His exposure to Western education and culture profoundly influenced his worldview, shaping his ideas about democracy, socialism, and secularism.

Involvement in the Freedom Struggle

AFTER RETURNING TO India in 1912, Nehru began practicing law in Allahabad. However, his interest in the Indian independence movement soon overshadowed his legal career. Inspired by the nationalist fervor and the leadership of Mahatma Gandhi, Nehru became increasingly involved in the struggle for freedom from British rule.

Nehru joined the Indian National Congress and quickly emerged as a prominent leader within the party. He was deeply influenced by Gandhi's philosophy of non-violence and civil disobedience, and he participated in several key movements, including the Non-Cooperation Movement in 1920 and the Civil Disobedience

Movement in 1930. Nehru's passion for India's independence and his commitment to social justice made him a popular leader among the masses.

Nehru's involvement in the freedom struggle also took him across the country, where he witnessed firsthand the poverty and suffering of the Indian people. This experience deeply affected him and strengthened his resolve to fight for a free and equitable India. Nehru's speeches and writings during this period reflect his deep commitment to the principles of equality, justice, and human dignity.

Role in the Indian National Congress

NEHRU'S LEADERSHIP within the Indian National Congress grew steadily during the 1920s and 1930s. He served as the party's president several times and played a key role in shaping its policies and strategies. Nehru was a strong advocate for complete independence from British rule, and he pushed the Congress to adopt a more radical stance in its demand for freedom.

In 1930, Nehru was arrested for participating in the Salt Satyagraha, a civil disobedience movement against the British salt tax. His imprisonment only increased his popularity and solidified his position as one of the foremost leaders of the independence movement. Throughout the 1930s and 1940s, Nehru continued to lead mass protests, rallies, and campaigns against British rule, often facing imprisonment and persecution.

Nehru's vision for India extended beyond independence. He was deeply committed to the idea of a secular, democratic, and socialist India. He believed in the importance of economic planning, industrialization, and scientific progress as means to achieve social and economic justice for all Indians. His ideas formed the basis of the Congress Party's platform in the years leading up to independence.

Independence and Partition

INDIA'S LONG STRUGGLE for independence finally culminated in 1947, with the end of British colonial rule. However, the joy of independence was marred by the painful and tragic partition of the country into India and Pakistan. The partition, based on religious lines, led to widespread communal violence, displacement, and suffering for millions of people.

As the newly appointed Prime Minister of India, Nehru faced the monumental task of leading the nation through this period of turmoil. He worked tirelessly to restore peace and order, provide relief to refugees, and rebuild the country's shattered economy. Nehru's leadership during this difficult time was marked by his deep empathy for the suffering of the people and his unwavering commitment to secularism and national unity.

Prime Ministerial Tenure

NEHRU'S TENURE AS PRIME Minister spanned 17 years, making him the longest-serving Prime Minister in Indian history. During this period, he implemented a wide range of policies and programs aimed at modernizing India and promoting social and economic development.

One of Nehru's key achievements was the establishment of a democratic political system in India. He oversaw the drafting and adoption of the Indian Constitution, which enshrined the principles of democracy, secularism, and fundamental rights. Nehru was a strong advocate of parliamentary democracy and believed in the importance of free and fair elections, the rule of law, and an independent judiciary.

Nehru also played a crucial role in shaping India's foreign policy. He was a proponent of non-alignment, a policy that sought to keep India independent of the major power blocs during the Cold War. Nehru's vision of non-alignment was rooted in his belief in peace, disarmament, and international cooperation. Under his leadership,

India emerged as a leading voice in the Non-Aligned Movement and played a significant role in international diplomacy.

Economic and Social Reforms

NEHRU'S VISION FOR India's economic development was based on the principles of socialism and planned economy. He believed that the state should play a central role in guiding economic development and ensuring social justice. Nehru's government implemented a series of Five-Year Plans, which focused on industrialization, agricultural development, and infrastructure building.

One of Nehru's most significant contributions was the establishment of a network of public sector enterprises, which laid the foundation for India's industrial base. He also prioritized the development of science and technology, leading to the creation of institutions like the Indian Institutes of Technology (IITs) and the Indian Space Research Organisation (ISRO). Nehru's emphasis on education and scientific research helped India make significant strides in these fields.

Nehru was also committed to social reforms, particularly in the areas of land redistribution, social justice, and women's rights. His government passed several laws aimed at abolishing feudal practices, promoting land reforms, and improving the status of women in society. Nehru was a strong advocate for women's education and empowerment, and he worked to ensure that women had equal rights and opportunities in independent India.

Challenges and Criticisms

DESPITE HIS MANY ACHIEVEMENTS, Nehru's tenure as Prime Minister was not without challenges and criticisms. One of the most significant challenges he faced was the Sino-Indian War in 1962, which resulted in a humiliating defeat for India. The war exposed weaknesses in India's defense preparedness and led to widespread criticism of Nehru's foreign policy, particularly his trust in China's intentions.

Nehru also faced criticism for his economic policies, particularly the slow pace of industrialization and the persistence of poverty and inequality in India. Some critics argued that Nehru's focus on heavy industry and public sector enterprises led to inefficiencies and stifled private enterprise. Others felt that his socialist policies did not do enough to address the needs of India's vast rural population.

Despite these challenges, Nehru remained deeply committed to his vision for India. He continued to work tirelessly for the country's development and progress until the end of his life.

Death and Legacy

JAWAHARLAL NEHRU PASSED away on May 27, 1964, leaving behind a legacy that continues to shape India to this day. His contributions to the nation as its first Prime Minister, his vision for a modern, democratic, and secular India, and his commitment to social justice and economic development have left an indelible mark on the country.

Nehru is remembered as the architect of modern India, a leader who laid the foundations for the nation's political, economic, and social institutions. His emphasis on democracy, secularism, and the rule of law has become an integral part of India's national identity. Nehru's vision of a united and inclusive India, where all citizens have the opportunity to thrive, remains a guiding principle for the country.

Nehru's legacy also lives on through the institutions he helped create, including the IITs, ISRO, and numerous public sector enterprises. His contributions to international diplomacy and the Non-Aligned Movement continue to be recognized globally.

Every year, Nehru's birthday, November 14, is celebrated as Children's Day in India, reflecting his deep love for children and his belief in the importance of nurturing the next generation.

Conclusion

JAWAHARLAL NEHRU'S tenure as India's first Prime Minister was a period of immense significance in the country's history. His leadership, vision, and policies laid the foundation for a modern, democratic, and inclusive India. Nehru's legacy as a statesman, a visionary, and a champion of social justice continues to inspire generations of Indians, and his contributions to the nation's development will be remembered for years to come.

Chapter 2:
Gulzarilal Nanda (1964 and 1966, Acting)

Gulzarilal Nanda is a name that often comes up in the context of the Indian political landscape, yet he remains a somewhat lesser-known figure compared to some of his more prominent contemporaries. Nanda served as the Acting Prime Minister of India twice—first in 1964, following the death of Jawaharlal Nehru, and again in 1966, after the death of Lal Bahadur Shastri. His brief tenures as Acting Prime Minister were marked by his calm and steady leadership during periods of national transition.

Birth and Early Life

GULZARILAL NANDA WAS born on July 4, 1898, in Sialkot, in what is now Pakistan. His father, Babu Bulaki Ram Aggarwal, was a school teacher, and Nanda grew up in a modest household. He pursued his early education in Lahore and Amritsar before attending the Foreman Christian College in Lahore, where he obtained his Master's degree in Economics.

Nanda's interest in social and economic issues developed early in his life, influenced by his academic background and his observations of the socio-economic conditions in India. He was particularly drawn to the ideas of Mahatma Gandhi and became involved in the Indian independence movement at a young age.

Involvement in the Freedom Struggle

NANDA'S ENTRY INTO the freedom struggle began in the 1920s, influenced by Mahatma Gandhi's principles of non-violence and civil disobedience. He joined the Indian National Congress and became actively involved in various movements against British colonial rule. Nanda participated in the Non-Cooperation Movement of 1920 and was imprisoned for his involvement in the Civil Disobedience Movement in 1932.

Nanda's commitment to social justice and economic reform was evident in his work during the freedom struggle. He focused on labor issues and became a prominent figure in the trade union movement. His dedication to improving the conditions of workers and advocating for their rights earned him a reputation as a compassionate and effective leader.

Political Career and Contributions

AFTER INDIA GAINED independence in 1947, Gulzarilal Nanda was appointed as the Minister for Labour in the interim government led by Jawaharlal Nehru. He played a crucial role in shaping labor policies in the newly independent nation. Nanda was instrumental in the passage of several important labor laws, including the Minimum Wages Act, 1948, which aimed to ensure fair wages for workers across various industries.

Nanda's expertise in labor and economic issues led to his appointment as the Planning Minister in Nehru's cabinet. He was closely involved in the formulation of India's Five-Year Plans, which aimed to promote industrialization, economic development, and social welfare. Nanda's work in this area reflected his deep commitment to improving the living standards of all Indians, particularly the working class.

First Term as Acting Prime Minister (1964)

GULZARILAL NANDA'S first term as Acting Prime Minister came under difficult circumstances. On May 27, 1964, India's first Prime Minister, Jawaharlal Nehru, passed away, leaving a leadership vacuum in the country. As the senior-most minister in the cabinet, Nanda was appointed as the Acting Prime Minister until the Congress Party could elect a new leader.

Nanda's brief tenure as Acting Prime Minister lasted from May 27 to June 9, 1964. During this period, he provided stable and calm leadership, ensuring that the government continued to function smoothly despite the shock of Nehru's death. Nanda's reputation for honesty, integrity, and dedication to public service helped reassure the nation during this period of uncertainty.

While Nanda's time as Acting Prime Minister was short, his contribution to maintaining stability in the country was significant. His ability to handle the responsibilities of the office with dignity and humility earned him respect from his colleagues and the public.

Second Term as Acting Prime Minister (1966)

GULZARILAL NANDA'S second term as Acting Prime Minister occurred under similarly challenging circumstances. On January 11, 1966, Prime Minister Lal Bahadur Shastri passed away unexpectedly in Tashkent, Uzbekistan, following the signing of the Tashkent Agreement with Pakistan. Once again, Nanda was called upon to step in as Acting Prime Minister.

Nanda's second term as Acting Prime Minister lasted from January 11 to January 24, 1966. During this period, he continued to provide steady leadership, ensuring that the transition of power was smooth and orderly. Nanda's experience and calm demeanor were particularly valuable during this time, as the country faced uncertainty and grief over the sudden loss of its leader.

Following Shastri's death, the Congress Party elected Indira Gandhi as the new Prime Minister, and Nanda once again stepped aside, returning to his role as a senior minister in the government.

Later Life and Legacy

AFTER HIS SECOND TERM as Acting Prime Minister, Gulzarilal Nanda continued to serve in various capacities within the Indian government. He remained active in public life, focusing on issues related to labor, social welfare, and economic development. Despite his significant contributions, Nanda never sought the limelight and preferred to work quietly and diligently for the betterment of the nation.

Nanda's legacy is one of humility, dedication, and service. He is remembered as a leader who stepped up during critical moments in India's history, providing stability and continuity in times of transition. His commitment to social justice, labor rights, and economic planning has left a lasting impact on the nation.

In recognition of his contributions to the country, Gulzarilal Nanda was awarded the Bharat Ratna, India's highest civilian honor, in

1997. He passed away on January 15, 1998, at the age of 99, leaving behind a legacy of integrity, service, and devotion to the nation.

Conclusion

GULZARILAL NANDA'S brief but crucial terms as Acting Prime Minister highlight his role as a stabilizing force in Indian politics during times of transition. His leadership, though often understated, was marked by a deep commitment to the principles of democracy, social justice, and public service. Nanda's life and career serve as an example of selfless leadership and dedication to the greater good, qualities that continue to inspire future generations of Indians.

LAL BAHADUR SHASTRI, India's second Prime Minister, was a leader of great integrity, simplicity, and dedication. Though his tenure as Prime Minister was brief, from 1964 to 1966, Shastri left an indelible mark on the country with his decisive leadership during one of the most challenging periods in India's post-independence chistory. He is best remembered for his leadership during the Indo-Pakistani War of

1965 and for coining the iconic slogan "Jai Jawan, Jai Kisan" ("Hail the Soldier, Hail the Farmer").

Birth and Early Life

LAL BAHADUR SHASTRI was born on October 2, 1904, in Mughalsarai, a small town in present-day Uttar Pradesh, India. His father, Sharada Prasad Srivastava, was a school teacher who passed away when Shastri was only a year old. His mother, Ramdulari Devi, raised him and his siblings under modest circumstances. The young Shastri was exposed to the values of humility, simplicity, and resilience from a very early age, traits that would define his personality and leadership style throughout his life.

Shastri's early education took place in Varanasi (then known as Benares). Even as a student, he was deeply influenced by the nationalist fervor that was sweeping through the country. At the age of 16, inspired by Mahatma Gandhi's call for non-cooperation against British rule, Shastri joined the freedom struggle, abandoning his studies to participate in the movement.

Education and Early Career

DESPITE LEAVING FORMAL education to join the independence movement, Shastri later pursued his studies at the Kashi Vidyapith in Varanasi, where he earned the title of "Shastri," meaning "scholar," as a mark of academic achievement. This title became so synonymous with him that it replaced his actual surname.

During the 1920s, Shastri became an active participant in the Indian National Congress and was closely associated with leaders like Mahatma Gandhi and Jawaharlal Nehru. He participated in various movements, including the Non-Cooperation Movement and the Salt Satyagraha, and was imprisoned several times by the British authorities. His years in prison only strengthened his resolve to fight for India's independence.

Political Career and Contributions

AFTER INDIA GAINED independence in 1947, Lal Bahadur Shastri became an integral part of the newly-formed government under Prime Minister Jawaharlal Nehru. He held several important positions in Nehru's cabinet, including Minister of Railways and Minister of Home Affairs. Shastri was known for his efficiency, integrity, and ability to handle complex issues with tact and determination.

As the Minister of Railways, Shastri introduced several key reforms, including improving the working conditions of railway employees and ensuring the welfare of passengers. He resigned from his position in 1956, taking moral responsibility for a railway accident in Tamil Nadu that resulted in many deaths. This gesture of accountability and ethical leadership earned him widespread respect.

As the Home Minister, Shastri played a crucial role in managing the internal security of the country. He was instrumental in handling the linguistic reorganization of states in India, a complex and sensitive issue that required careful negotiation and diplomacy.

Becoming Prime Minister

FOLLOWING THE DEATH of Jawaharlal Nehru in May 1964, Lal Bahadur Shastri was chosen by the Congress Party to succeed him as Prime Minister. Shastri's selection as Prime Minister was not without challenges; he was seen as a consensus candidate who could unite the party's various factions. Despite being relatively modest and unassuming, Shastri's deep understanding of India's socio-political landscape and his ability to command respect across party lines made him the ideal choice for the leadership.

Leadership during the Indo-Pakistani War of 1965

ONE OF THE MOST DEFINING moments of Lal Bahadur Shastri's tenure as Prime Minister was the Indo-Pakistani War of 1965.

The conflict, which arose over territorial disputes in the Rann of Kutch and later in Kashmir, tested Shastri's leadership and resolve.

Shastri responded to the challenge with firmness and determination. He emphasized the importance of national security and rallied the country with the slogan "Jai Jawan, Jai Kisan," which highlighted the critical roles of soldiers and farmers in defending and sustaining the nation. The slogan resonated deeply with the Indian public, galvanizing the nation to support the war effort.

Under Shastri's leadership, the Indian military performed admirably, and the war ended with the signing of the Tashkent Agreement on January 10, 1966, a peace treaty between India and Pakistan mediated by the Soviet Union. Although the agreement aimed to restore peace, it did not fully resolve the underlying issues between the two countries. Nevertheless, Shastri's handling of the war and the subsequent negotiations enhanced his reputation as a leader who could protect India's interests on the global stage.

Economic and Social Initiatives

IN ADDITION TO HIS leadership during the war, Shastri focused on addressing India's economic challenges. He recognized the importance of agriculture in India's economy and took steps to boost food production, particularly during a time of severe food shortages. Shastri encouraged the adoption of modern agricultural techniques and supported the Green Revolution, which eventually led to increased crop yields and greater food security for the country.

Shastri also worked to strengthen India's economic policies, focusing on self-reliance and reducing dependence on foreign aid. His policies were aimed at fostering economic growth while maintaining social equity, a balance that he believed was essential for India's long-term stability and development.

Death and Legacy

LAL BAHADUR SHASTRI'S tenure as Prime Minister was tragically cut short by his sudden death on January 11, 1966, in Tashkent, Uzbekistan, just a day after signing the Tashkent Agreement. The circumstances of his death remain the subject of speculation and controversy, with some theories suggesting foul play, though no conclusive evidence has ever been found.

Shastri's death was a significant loss for India, as the nation mourned a leader who embodied the values of honesty, humility, and dedication to public service. Despite his short tenure, Shastri left a profound legacy that continues to inspire generations of Indians.

Shastri is remembered as a leader who led by example, placing the interests of the nation above personal or political considerations. His commitment to the welfare of both the soldier and the farmer—two pillars of India's strength—remains a guiding principle for the country. The "Jai Jawan, Jai Kisan" slogan continues to be a powerful reminder of the importance of unity, hard work, and patriotism.

In honor of his contributions to the nation, several institutions, roads, and public spaces have been named after Lal Bahadur Shastri. His birthplace, Mughalsarai, was renamed "Deen Dayal Upadhyay Nagar" in his memory, and the Lal Bahadur Shastri National Academy of Administration (LBSNAA) in Mussoorie, where India's civil servants are trained, stands as a testament to his enduring influence.

Conclusion

LAL BAHADUR SHASTRI'S time as Prime Minister, though brief, was marked by decisive leadership and a deep commitment to the values that define India. His ability to lead the country through war, address economic challenges, and uphold the principles of democracy and social justice earned him a place of great respect in the annals of Indian history. Shastri's life and leadership continue to serve as an example of what it means to lead with integrity, humility, and a sense of duty to the nation.

INDIRA GANDHI, THE first and only woman to serve as the Prime Minister of India, was a towering figure in Indian politics. Her tenure from 1966 to 1977 marked a period of significant political and social change in the country. Known for her strong leadership and decisive actions, Indira Gandhi left a profound impact on India's political landscape. Her leadership was characterized by both remarkable achievements and controversial decisions, making her one of the most polarizing figures in Indian history.

Early Life and Background

INDIRA PRIYADARSHINI Gandhi was born on November 19, 1917, in Allahabad, Uttar Pradesh, into one of India's most prominent political families. She was the daughter of Jawaharlal Nehru, India's first Prime Minister, and Kamala Nehru. Growing up in the Nehru household, Indira was exposed to politics from a very young age, often interacting with leaders of the Indian independence movement.

Indira's education was eclectic and international. She attended schools in India, Switzerland, and the United Kingdom, including the prestigious Somerville College, Oxford. Her time in Europe, particularly during the tumultuous years leading up to World War II, exposed her to various political ideologies and shaped her understanding of global politics.

Indira married Feroze Gandhi in 1942, and the couple had two sons, Rajiv and Sanjay. Despite her domestic responsibilities, Indira remained actively involved in politics, often assisting her father in his work and gradually emerging as a significant figure in the Indian National Congress.

Rise to Power

INDIRA GANDHI'S FORMAL entry into politics came in the late 1950s when she was elected President of the Indian National Congress. Her leadership in the party, coupled with her close association with her father, positioned her as a key player in Indian politics. After Nehru's death in 1964, Lal Bahadur Shastri became Prime Minister, and Indira was appointed as the Minister of Information and Broadcasting, a significant role that allowed her to build her political credentials.

Shastri's sudden death in January 1966 created a power vacuum in the Congress Party. Indira Gandhi emerged as a compromise candidate for the Prime Minister's position, largely because senior leaders believed she would be easily controlled. However, once in power, Indira quickly asserted her authority, surprising many with her political acumen and determination.

Major Policies and Initiatives

INDIRA GANDHI'S FIRST term as Prime Minister was marked by a series of bold and transformative policies. One of her most significant achievements was the nationalization of banks in 1969. This move was part of her broader strategy to consolidate economic power and reduce the influence of private capital in the country's financial system. The bank nationalization not only increased the government's control over the economy but also aligned Indira with the socialist policies of her father.

Another major policy during her early years as Prime Minister was the abolition of the privy purses and privileges of former princely states. This decision, which stripped the erstwhile rulers of their financial privileges, was seen as a move to further democratize Indian society and reduce the remnants of feudalism.

The Green Revolution

ONE OF INDIRA GANDHI'S most enduring legacies is the Green Revolution, a series of initiatives aimed at increasing agricultural production in India. Facing severe food shortages and the threat of famine, Indira's government introduced high-yielding varieties of seeds, modern irrigation techniques, and fertilizers to boost crop production, particularly in wheat and rice.

The Green Revolution transformed India from a food-deficient country to one that was largely self-sufficient in grain production. This agricultural success not only secured Indira Gandhi's political position but also alleviated the chronic food insecurity that had plagued India for decades. However, the Green Revolution also had its critics, who pointed out its environmental impact and the increased economic disparity it created between different regions and social classes.

The Indo-Pakistani War of 1971 and the Creation of Bangladesh

INDIRA GANDHI'S LEADERSHIP during the Indo-Pakistani War of 1971 is often considered one of her finest moments. The conflict arose from the crisis in East Pakistan (now Bangladesh), where a brutal crackdown by the Pakistani military on Bengali nationalists led to widespread atrocities and a massive refugee influx into India.

Indira Gandhi's decision to support the Bengali independence movement and her subsequent military intervention in East Pakistan were decisive. The war, which lasted just 13 days, ended in a comprehensive victory for India and the creation of the independent state of Bangladesh. This success greatly enhanced Indira's stature both domestically and internationally, establishing her as a powerful leader on the global stage.

The Emergency (1975–1977)

DESPITE HER MANY ACHIEVEMENTS, Indira Gandhi's legacy is deeply marred by her decision to impose a state of Emergency in India from June 25, 1975, to March 21, 1977. The Emergency was declared in response to growing political opposition and a court ruling that found her guilty of electoral malpractice, which threatened her position as Prime Minister.

During the Emergency, Indira Gandhi suspended civil liberties, censored the press, and arrested political opponents. The period was marked by widespread human rights abuses, including forced sterilizations and the demolition of slums in urban areas. The Emergency is often viewed as the darkest chapter of Indira Gandhi's political career, reflecting her increasingly authoritarian approach to governance.

The widespread discontent with the Emergency policies led to Indira's downfall in the 1977 general elections, where the Congress Party suffered a massive defeat, and the Janata Party, a coalition of opposition groups, came to power.

Conclusion

INDIRA GANDHI'S FIRST tenure as Prime Minister from 1966 to 1977 was a period of intense political activity and transformation for India. Her leadership saw the country through both triumphs and crises, and her decisions left a lasting impact on India's socio-political fabric. While her policies like the Green Revolution and her role in the creation of Bangladesh are celebrated, the imposition of the Emergency casts a long shadow over her legacy. Indira Gandhi remains a complex figure in Indian history, remembered both for her contributions to the nation and the controversies that marked her time in power.

MORARJI DESAI HOLDS the distinction of being India's first non-Congress Prime Minister, serving from 1977 to 1979. His tenure marked a significant shift in Indian politics, as it represented the first time a coalition government took power at the center, ending the long-standing dominance of the Indian National Congress. Desai's leadership was characterized by his commitment to discipline, moral integrity, and a strict adherence to Gandhian principles, particularly in areas of governance and personal conduct.

Early Life and Background

MORARJI RANCHHODJI Desai was born on February 29, 1896, in Bhadeli, a small village in the Bulsar district of Gujarat. He came from a family deeply rooted in the values of honesty, simplicity, and service, which had a profound influence on his character and worldview. Desai pursued his education at the University of Bombay (now Mumbai), where he earned a degree in arts before joining the civil services in the then Bombay Province.

Desai's career in the British Indian civil service was marked by his commitment to discipline and efficiency. However, the call of the freedom movement, led by Mahatma Gandhi, eventually drew him away from his bureaucratic career. In 1930, he resigned from his position to join the Indian National Congress and actively participate in the struggle for independence.

Involvement in the Freedom Struggle

MORARJI DESAI WAS AN ardent follower of Mahatma Gandhi and played an active role in the civil disobedience movement and the Quit India Movement. His commitment to non-violence and his deep belief in the principles of Satyagraha made him a trusted lieutenant of Gandhi. Desai was imprisoned several times by the British authorities for his participation in these movements, which only strengthened his resolve to fight for India's independence.

Political Career Post-Independence

AFTER INDIA GAINED independence in 1947, Desai quickly rose through the ranks of the Indian National Congress. He served as the Chief Minister of Bombay State from 1952 to 1956, where he earned a reputation for his administrative efficiency and integrity. His tenure was marked by efforts to modernize the state's economy and improve public services, particularly in education and health.

Desai's success in Bombay led to his appointment as a minister in the central government. He held several key portfolios, including finance, home affairs, and agriculture, where his policies were often driven by his belief in self-discipline and economic austerity. As Finance Minister, Desai was known for his conservative fiscal policies, focusing on controlling inflation and maintaining strict budgetary discipline.

Break with the Congress and the Rise of the Janata Party

DESAI'S POLITICAL CAREER took a dramatic turn in the late 1960s when he clashed with Prime Minister Indira Gandhi. The differences between them were not just ideological but also personal, as Desai believed in a strict adherence to party rules and was critical of what he saw as Indira Gandhi's authoritarian tendencies. The split culminated in Desai's ouster from the Congress leadership and his decision to join the opposition.

The imposition of the Emergency by Indira Gandhi in 1975 was a turning point for Desai and many others who opposed her. During the Emergency, Desai was arrested and imprisoned along with other political leaders. However, the widespread discontent with the Emergency policies led to the formation of the Janata Party, a coalition of opposition groups, which united to challenge Indira Gandhi's rule.

Prime Ministership (1977–1979)

IN THE 1977 GENERAL elections, the Janata Party won a decisive victory, and Morarji Desai was chosen as the Prime Minister, making him the first non-Congress leader to hold the office. His government was marked by a commitment to restoring democratic norms, which had been severely undermined during the Emergency.

One of the first actions taken by Desai's government was to repeal many of the laws and ordinances enacted during the Emergency. His administration also focused on rolling back censorship and restoring civil liberties. Desai was determined to ensure that such a period of authoritarian rule would not be repeated in India.

In foreign policy, Desai pursued a policy of non-alignment, maintaining India's independence in international affairs. He worked to improve relations with neighboring countries, including Pakistan, with whom he sought to resolve ongoing tensions through diplomatic means.

However, Desai's tenure was not without challenges. The coalition government he led was marked by internal divisions and conflicts between various factions of the Janata Party. These differences often hampered the government's ability to implement its policies effectively. Additionally, Desai's strict moral and economic conservatism sometimes alienated members of his own party and the general public.

Later Life and Legacy

DESAI'S GOVERNMENT eventually fell in 1979 due to internal dissent and the withdrawal of support by key coalition partners. After stepping down as Prime Minister, Desai retired from active politics, although he continued to be involved in public life, advocating for issues close to his heart, such as prohibition and the promotion of traditional Indian values.

Morarji Desai's legacy is one of principled leadership and commitment to democratic ideals. He was awarded the Bharat Ratna, India's highest civilian honor, in 1991, in recognition of his contributions to the nation. Desai passed away on April 10, 1995, at the age of 99.

Desai is remembered as a leader who, despite his conservative approach, played a crucial role in steering India through a critical phase in its history. His dedication to moral integrity, discipline, and democratic governance continues to be admired, even as his tenure as Prime Minister is often viewed through the lens of the challenges and limitations he faced in managing a coalition government.

Chapter 6

Charan Singh (1979–1980)

CHARAN SINGH, INDIA'S Prime Minister from 1979 to 1980, was a prominent political figure known for his deep connection with rural India and his advocacy for the rights of farmers. Often referred to as the "Champion of Indian Peasantry," Singh's policies and leadership were heavily influenced by his agrarian roots and his belief that India's true strength lay in its villages. His brief tenure as Prime Minister was marked by political instability, but his legacy as a leader who fought for the agricultural community remains significant in Indian history.

Early Life and Background

CHARAN SINGH WAS BORN on December 23, 1902, in the small village of Noorpur in the Meerut district of Uttar Pradesh. He hailed from a Jat family, a community traditionally involved in agriculture, which profoundly influenced his worldview. Singh grew up witnessing the struggles of farmers and the exploitation they often faced at the hands of landlords and the colonial administration.

He was a bright student and pursued his higher education at Agra University, where he earned a master's degree in arts and a law degree. Singh began his career as a lawyer, practicing at the district court in Ghaziabad. However, his deep-seated desire to address the issues faced by farmers drew him into politics.

Entry into Politics and Advocacy for Farmers

CHARAN SINGH'S ENTRY into politics was rooted in his commitment to agrarian reform and social justice. He joined the Indian National Congress and became actively involved in the freedom movement. Singh was particularly influenced by Mahatma Gandhi's emphasis on self-reliance and rural development, which aligned with his own beliefs.

In the 1930s and 1940s, Singh emerged as a strong voice for farmers in Uttar Pradesh. He was instrumental in drafting and advocating for several pieces of legislation aimed at protecting the rights of tenant farmers and ensuring fair land distribution. His most notable contribution during this period was the formulation of the Uttar Pradesh Zamindari Abolition and Land Reforms Act, 1950, which sought to abolish the feudal landholding system and redistribute land to the tillers.

Political Career Post-Independence

AFTER INDIA GAINED independence in 1947, Charan Singh continued his political career with a focus on agrarian issues. He held various ministerial positions in the Uttar Pradesh state government, including Minister of Agriculture and later, Chief Minister. Singh's policies as Chief Minister were aimed at improving the lives of farmers and rural communities, with a focus on land reforms, irrigation, and agricultural development.

Singh's growing influence in Uttar Pradesh politics eventually led him to the national stage. He became a prominent leader in the Congress Party, particularly within its rural faction. However, Singh's differences with the central leadership, particularly with Prime Minister Indira Gandhi, led to a split. He opposed Indira Gandhi's socialist policies, which he believed were detrimental to the agricultural sector and rural communities.

Formation of the Bharatiya Lok Dal and Role in the Janata Party

IN THE 1960S, CHARAN Singh broke away from the Congress Party and formed his own political outfit, the Bharatiya Kranti Dal, which later became the Bharatiya Lok Dal. His party primarily represented the interests of farmers and rural communities, and Singh became the voice of agrarian India.

The political landscape in India underwent significant changes during the Emergency period (1975–1977) imposed by Indira Gandhi. Singh was a vocal critic of the Emergency and was arrested along with other opposition leaders. His opposition to Indira Gandhi's authoritarian rule solidified his standing as a leader of the masses, particularly in the Hindi-speaking belt of North India.

In the 1977 general elections, following the lifting of the Emergency, Charan Singh played a crucial role in the formation of the Janata Party, a coalition of opposition parties that came together to defeat Indira Gandhi's Congress. The Janata Party won a decisive victory, and Singh was appointed as the Deputy Prime Minister and Minister of Home Affairs in Morarji Desai's government.

Prime Ministership (1979–1980)

CHARAN SINGH'S ASCENSION to the position of Prime Minister came amidst internal conflicts within the Janata Party. Disagreements between Morarji Desai and Singh, along with factionalism within the party, led to Desai's resignation in 1979. Singh was then chosen as the Prime Minister, with the support of a section of the Janata Party and the Congress Party under Indira Gandhi, who saw an opportunity to destabilize the government.

However, Singh's tenure as Prime Minister was short-lived. He assumed office on July 28, 1979, but the Congress Party, which had promised external support to his government, withdrew it before he could even face a vote of confidence in Parliament. As a result, Singh was forced to resign on January 14, 1980, after just 170 days in office. His brief tenure as Prime Minister was marked by political instability and his inability to push through significant policy changes due to the lack of a stable majority.

Later Life and Legacy

AFTER RESIGNING AS Prime Minister, Charan Singh continued to be an influential figure in Indian politics, particularly in Uttar Pradesh. He remained a vocal advocate for farmers' rights and agrarian issues, though his political influence waned in the face of a resurgent Congress Party under Indira Gandhi.

Charan Singh passed away on May 29, 1987, leaving behind a legacy as a staunch defender of the rural poor and a leader who remained deeply connected to the land and its people. His contributions to land reforms and his efforts to bring the concerns of farmers to the forefront of national politics have had a lasting impact on Indian society.

In recognition of his contributions, the government of India named several institutions and places after him, including the Chaudhary Charan Singh International Airport in Lucknow and the Charan Singh University in Meerut. His legacy continues to be celebrated, particularly in the rural heartland of North India, where he is remembered as a leader who championed the cause of the common farmer.

Chapter 7:
Indira Gandhi (1980–1984)

INDIRA GANDHI, ONE of India's most influential and controversial leaders, returned to power as Prime Minister in 1980 after a period of political turmoil. Her second tenure, lasting from 1980 until her assassination in 1984, was marked by significant achievements, as well as challenges and controversies that have left a lasting impact on Indian politics and society.

Return to Power

INDIRA GANDHI'S RETURN to power in 1980 was a remarkable political comeback. After the defeat of her government in the 1977 general elections and the subsequent political challenges she faced, including her arrest and the split within the Congress Party, many believed her political career was over. However, her resilience and political acumen allowed her to stage a comeback. The political instability and internal divisions within the Janata Party government led to its downfall, and in the 1980 general elections, the Congress (I) Party, led by Indira Gandhi, won a sweeping victory. Her return to power marked the beginning of a new chapter in Indian politics.

Major Policies and Initiatives

DURING HER SECOND TERM, Indira Gandhi focused on strengthening India's economic and military capabilities, while also addressing the pressing social issues of the time. She continued with her earlier policies of nationalization and state control over key industries, although she also initiated efforts to modernize India's economy.

One of the key initiatives of her government was the "20-Point Programme," aimed at alleviating poverty and improving the quality of life for the poor. The program focused on areas such as land reforms, rural development, health, education, and social welfare. Although the implementation of these initiatives was uneven, they highlighted her commitment to addressing the needs of the marginalized sections of society.

Indira Gandhi also placed a strong emphasis on national security and defense. In response to increasing threats from neighboring countries and internal security challenges, she strengthened India's military capabilities, including the expansion of the nuclear program. Her government also undertook significant modernization of the armed forces.

Operation Blue Star

ONE OF THE MOST CONTROVERSIAL and consequential decisions of Indira Gandhi's second term was the launch of "Operation Blue Star" in 1984. The operation was a military action ordered by her government to remove Sikh militants, led by Jarnail Singh Bhindranwale, who had fortified themselves in the Golden Temple in Amritsar, Punjab. The militants were demanding the creation of an independent Sikh state, known as Khalistan.

The decision to send the army into the Golden Temple, one of the holiest sites in Sikhism, was met with widespread criticism and led to significant unrest in Punjab and among the global Sikh community. The operation resulted in the deaths of many militants, soldiers, and civilians, and the damage to the Golden Temple further fueled anger and resentment. While the government justified the operation as necessary to maintain law and order, it left a deep scar on India's political and social fabric, and it significantly strained Hindu-Sikh relations.

Assassination and Legacy

INDIRA GANDHI'S DECISION to launch Operation Blue Star had dire personal consequences. On October 31, 1984, she was assassinated by two of her Sikh bodyguards in retaliation for the operation. Her assassination triggered widespread anti-Sikh riots across the country, particularly in Delhi, where thousands of Sikhs were killed in the ensuing violence. The events of 1984 remain a dark chapter in India's history, with long-lasting implications for communal harmony and justice.

Despite the controversies that marked her leadership, Indira Gandhi's legacy as a strong, determined, and charismatic leader endures. She is remembered for her significant contributions to India's development, particularly in terms of economic modernization, social welfare, and strengthening national security. Her leadership during the

1971 Bangladesh Liberation War, which resulted in the creation of Bangladesh, is one of her most celebrated achievements.

Indira Gandhi's tenure also left a lasting impact on the structure of Indian politics. She centralized power within the office of the Prime Minister and within the Congress Party, a move that has been both praised for ensuring decisive governance and criticized for weakening democratic institutions. Her political style, often described as authoritarian, has been a subject of intense debate among historians and political analysts.

Indira Gandhi remains one of the most complex and polarizing figures in Indian history. Her leadership style, decisions, and policies continue to influence Indian politics, and she is often studied as an example of the challenges and responsibilities of leadership in a diverse and populous democracy.

RAJIV GANDHI, THE YOUNGEST Prime Minister in India's history, assumed office under tragic circumstances following the assassination of his mother, Indira Gandhi, in 1984. His tenure, from 1984 to 1989, was marked by a mix of modernizing reforms, efforts to stabilize a nation in mourning, and controversies that ultimately shaped his political legacy.

Early Life and Background

RAJIV GANDHI WAS BORN on August 20, 1944, in Bombay (now Mumbai) to Indira Gandhi and Feroze Gandhi. As the grandson of India's first Prime Minister, Jawaharlal Nehru, Rajiv grew up in the political spotlight, though he initially showed little interest in a political career. He attended the Doon School and later went on to study at Trinity College, Cambridge, and Imperial College, London, where he studied engineering, though he did not complete his degree.

In 1968, Rajiv married Sonia Maino, an Italian-born woman who would later become a significant figure in Indian politics. The couple preferred a relatively quiet life, and Rajiv pursued a career as a commercial pilot with Indian Airlines. His younger brother, Sanjay Gandhi, was initially seen as Indira Gandhi's political heir, but after Sanjay's untimely death in a plane crash in 1980, Rajiv was reluctantly drawn into the political arena.

Entry into Politics

FOLLOWING SANJAY'S death, Rajiv was persuaded by his mother and other Congress leaders to enter politics to help support her during a tumultuous period. He won a by-election to his brother's parliamentary seat in Amethi, Uttar Pradesh, and quickly became a key figure in the Indian National Congress.

Rajiv's entry into politics was marked by his initial reluctance and the perception that he was unprepared for the rough-and-tumble world of Indian politics. However, he soon demonstrated a pragmatic approach and a vision for modernizing India, focusing particularly on science, technology, and communication.

Becoming Prime Minister

THE ASSASSINATION OF Indira Gandhi on October 31, 1984, thrust Rajiv Gandhi into the highest office of the land. He was sworn in as Prime Minister the same day, amidst a wave of grief and violence, as anti-Sikh riots erupted across the country in retaliation for his mother's assassination by her Sikh bodyguards. Rajiv Gandhi's immediate challenge was to restore peace and order in the country, a task that was complicated by the widespread communal violence that followed.

In the general elections held in December 1984, Rajiv Gandhi led the Congress Party to a landslide victory, winning 414 out of 533 seats in the Lok Sabha, the largest majority ever secured in the Indian Parliament. This massive mandate gave him the opportunity to implement his vision for India, which centered on modernization, technological advancement, and economic reform.

Reforms and Modernization

RAJIV GANDHI'S TENURE as Prime Minister was characterized by a strong push towards modernizing India's economy and infrastructure. He is often credited with initiating the process of economic liberalization in India, laying the groundwork for the major economic reforms that would follow in the 1990s.

One of his key initiatives was the introduction of policies to promote the use of computers and telecommunications, which were still in their infancy in India. Rajiv recognized the potential of information technology and worked to create an environment that encouraged its growth. He established the Centre for Development of Telematics (C-DOT) and pushed for the expansion of telephone networks across the country.

Rajiv Gandhi also sought to reform the government bureaucracy, reduce red tape, and decentralize power. His government introduced the 64th Amendment Bill, aimed at strengthening Panchayati Raj institutions (local self-governments) to empower rural communities. Although the bill faced resistance and was not fully realized during his tenure, it set the stage for future reforms in local governance.

Foreign Policy and National Security

IN FOREIGN POLICY, Rajiv Gandhi continued India's commitment to non-alignment, but he also sought to strengthen India's global standing by improving relations with both the Soviet Union and the United States. He advocated for disarmament and played a role in promoting peace in international forums, including the United Nations.

Rajiv's government faced significant challenges on the national security front, particularly in dealing with insurgencies and separatist movements. In Punjab, the Khalistan movement continued to pose a threat, and in Sri Lanka, the civil war between the Tamil minority and the Sinhalese majority led to Indian involvement. Rajiv Gandhi's decision to send the Indian Peace Keeping Force (IPKF) to Sri Lanka in 1987 to enforce a peace accord between the warring factions was a controversial move. The IPKF became embroiled in a protracted conflict, leading to significant casualties and criticism of Rajiv's handling of the situation.

Controversies and Decline

DESPITE HIS INITIAL popularity and the sweeping mandate he received, Rajiv Gandhi's tenure was marred by several controversies that ultimately led to his political decline. The most damaging of these was the Bofors scandal, which broke in 1987. The scandal involved allegations that top government officials and Congress Party members had received kickbacks in a deal to purchase howitzer guns from the Swedish company Bofors. Although Rajiv Gandhi denied any involvement, the scandal severely tarnished his image and eroded public trust in his leadership.

The Shah Bano case in 1985 was another significant controversy during Rajiv's tenure. The case involved a Muslim woman, Shah Bano, who had been awarded alimony by the Supreme Court after being divorced by her husband. Rajiv Gandhi's government, under pressure from conservative Muslim groups, passed legislation to overturn the court's decision, leading to widespread criticism that he was appeasing religious minorities at the expense of women's rights.

These controversies, combined with growing dissatisfaction over the handling of insurgencies in Punjab and Kashmir, led to a decline in Rajiv Gandhi's popularity. In the 1989 general elections, the Congress Party lost its majority, and Rajiv Gandhi was succeeded by V.P. Singh as Prime Minister.

Assassination and Legacy

AFTER LOSING POWER, Rajiv Gandhi remained active in politics and was preparing for a political comeback when he was tragically assassinated on May 21, 1991, during an election rally in Sriperumbudur, Tamil Nadu. He was killed by a suicide bomber from the Liberation Tigers of Tamil Eelam (LTTE), a militant organization from Sri Lanka, in retaliation for his role in sending the IPKF to Sri Lanka.

Rajiv Gandhi's assassination shocked the nation and marked the end of an era in Indian politics. He was posthumously awarded the Bharat Ratna, India's highest civilian honor, in recognition of his contributions to the country.

Rajiv Gandhi's legacy is complex. He is remembered as a forward-looking leader who sought to modernize India and bring it into the 21st century. His emphasis on technology, education, and communication has had a lasting impact on India's development. However, his tenure was also marked by significant challenges and controversies that continue to be debated. His efforts to liberalize the economy and his push for technological advancement laid the foundation for the economic growth that India experienced in the subsequent decades. Rajiv Gandhi remains a pivotal figure in Indian history, representing both the aspirations and the challenges of a rapidly changing nation.

Chapter 9

Vishwanath Pratap Singh (1989–1990)

VISHWANATH PRATAP SINGH, popularly known as V.P. Singh, served as the Prime Minister of India from December 1989 to November 1990. His short tenure was marked by significant political and social upheavals, as well as his controversial decision to implement the Mandal Commission's recommendations, which fundamentally altered the landscape of Indian politics.

Early Life and Education

VISHWANATH PRATAP SINGH was born on June 25, 1931, in the royal family of Manda, near Allahabad, in the state of Uttar Pradesh. He was adopted by the Raja of Manda, which gave him the title of Raja. Singh received his early education at Colvin Taluqdars' College in Lucknow and then at the Allahabad University, where he earned a degree in science and law. Despite his aristocratic background, Singh was drawn to public service and joined the Congress Party, embarking on a political career that would see him rise to the highest office in the country.

Political Career Before Becoming Prime Minister

V.P. SINGH ENTERED politics in the 1960s, initially serving as a member of the Uttar Pradesh Legislative Assembly. He was elected to the Lok Sabha, the lower house of India's Parliament, in 1971, representing the constituency of Phulpur, a seat once held by Jawaharlal Nehru. Singh quickly gained a reputation as an honest and efficient administrator, which led to his appointment as the Chief Minister of Uttar Pradesh in 1980.

During his brief tenure as Chief Minister, Singh took a strong stand against corruption and worked to implement land reforms, which earned him both praise and criticism. He soon moved to the national stage, where he was appointed as the Minister of Commerce in Indira Gandhi's government. His work in the commerce ministry further bolstered his reputation as a clean and capable leader.

Finance Minister and Defense Minister

WHEN RAJIV GANDHI BECAME Prime Minister in 1984, he appointed V.P. Singh as the Finance Minister. In this role, Singh was instrumental in initiating a series of tax reforms aimed at curbing tax evasion and increasing government revenue. He also introduced measures to modernize India's financial sector and promote industrial growth.

However, it was his tenure as Defense Minister that brought him into conflict with Rajiv Gandhi and eventually led to his resignation from the Congress Party. In 1987, Singh began investigating allegations of corruption in defense procurement deals, most notably the Bofors scandal, which involved kickbacks in the purchase of artillery guns from the Swedish company Bofors. His insistence on transparency and accountability led to tensions with the Prime Minister and other senior Congress leaders. In 1987, Singh resigned from the cabinet and later left the Congress Party, positioning himself as a leader of the opposition.

Becoming Prime Minister

IN THE 1989 GENERAL elections, V.P. Singh emerged as a key figure in the opposition, leading the Janata Dal, a coalition of several political parties. The Congress Party, led by Rajiv Gandhi, suffered a significant defeat, and the Janata Dal, with the support of other opposition parties, including the Bharatiya Janata Party (BJP) and the Left Front, formed the government. On December 2, 1989, V.P. Singh was sworn in as the 8th Prime Minister of India.

Mandal Commission and Social Justice

V.P. SINGH'S TENURE as Prime Minister is most remembered for his decision to implement the recommendations of the Mandal Commission, a government commission established in 1979 to identify socially and educationally backward classes in India and recommend measures to improve their status. The commission had recommended that 27% of government jobs and seats in public universities be reserved for Other Backward Classes (OBCs).

In August 1990, V.P. Singh announced the implementation of these recommendations, a move that sparked widespread protests and controversy across the country. The decision was seen as a major step towards social justice and empowerment for historically marginalized communities, but it also led to significant opposition from those who felt that it would increase social divisions and undermine meritocracy.

The Mandal Commission's implementation led to a wave of protests, particularly among upper-caste students, some of whom resorted to self-immolation in a tragic display of opposition. The country was deeply divided over the issue, and the political fallout was immense.

Political Challenges and Downfall

V.P. SINGH'S DECISION to implement the Mandal Commission's recommendations created a rift within his own government and the coalition that supported it. The Bharatiya Janata Party (BJP), which had initially supported the Janata Dal government, began to distance itself from Singh, particularly over the issue of the Ram Janmabhoomi movement, which sought to build a temple at the disputed site in Ayodhya.

The BJP's decision to withdraw support from the government in November 1990, following Singh's refusal to accede to their demands regarding the Ayodhya issue, led to a vote of no confidence in Parliament. Unable to muster enough support, V.P. Singh resigned as Prime Minister on November 7, 1990, after serving for less than a year.

Legacy and Later Life

VISHWANATH PRATAP SINGH'S tenure as Prime Minister, though brief, had a profound impact on Indian society and politics. His decision to implement the Mandal Commission's recommendations is often cited as a turning point in Indian politics, leading to the rise of caste-based politics and the empowerment of OBC communities. This decision also contributed to the fragmentation of Indian politics, with the rise of regional parties and the decline of the Congress Party's dominance.

After resigning as Prime Minister, V.P. Singh continued to be an influential figure in Indian politics, although he never held office again. He became a symbol of social justice and continued to advocate for the rights of the underprivileged. Singh also remained a critic of corruption and authoritarianism in government.

Vishwanath Pratap Singh passed away on November 27, 2008, after a prolonged battle with multiple health issues, including cancer and renal failure. He is remembered as a leader who stood by his principles, even at the cost of his political career. His legacy is one of integrity, social justice, and a commitment to addressing the deep-rooted inequalities in Indian society. His tenure as Prime Minister, though short, left an indelible mark on the nation's political landscape.

CHANDRA SHEKHAR, OFTEN referred to as the "Young Turk" of Indian politics, served as the Prime Minister of India from November 1990 to June 1991. His tenure, though brief, was marked by significant political turbulence and economic challenges. Despite leading a minority government, Chandra Shekhar's commitment to his principles and his vision for a more equitable India left a lasting impression on the nation's political history.

Early Life and Education

CHANDRA SHEKHAR WAS born on July 1, 1927, in Ibrahimpatti, a small village in Ballia district, Uttar Pradesh. He came from a humble, farming background, which deeply influenced his worldview and his later political beliefs. Chandra Shekhar completed his early education in Ballia and later attended Allahabad University, where he earned a degree in political science. It was during his time at university that he became involved in politics, joining the socialist movement led by Jayaprakash Narayan, which advocated for social justice, economic equality, and a more decentralized form of governance.

Early Political Career

CHANDRA SHEKHAR'S POLITICAL career began in the 1950s when he joined the Indian National Congress. He was elected to the Rajya Sabha, the upper house of India's Parliament, in 1962. As a member of the Congress, he quickly gained a reputation as a firebrand leader, often challenging the party leadership on issues related to socialism and economic policies. His association with the "Young Turks" within the Congress—a group of young leaders who advocated for more radical economic and social reforms—cemented his image as a leader committed to the principles of socialism and social justice.

In 1969, Chandra Shekhar played a key role in supporting Indira Gandhi during the Congress Party's split, aligning himself with her faction, which came to be known as the Congress (R). Despite this, he remained an independent thinker, often at odds with Indira Gandhi's policies, particularly during the Emergency of 1975-1977. His vocal opposition to the Emergency, which he viewed as an authoritarian move that stifled democracy, led to his arrest and detention, further solidifying his reputation as a leader who stood by his principles.

Formation of the Janata Party

FOLLOWING THE EMERGENCY, Chandra Shekhar left the Congress Party and became one of the founding members of the Janata Party, a coalition of parties opposed to Indira Gandhi's rule. The Janata Party came to power in 1977, ending the long-standing dominance of the Congress Party. Chandra Shekhar served as the president of the Janata Party from 1977 to 1988, playing a crucial role in shaping the party's policies and strategies.

However, the Janata Party government, led by Morarji Desai, was short-lived, plagued by internal conflicts and a lack of cohesive leadership. Chandra Shekhar continued to be an influential figure in Indian politics, advocating for policies that would address the needs of India's poor and marginalized communities.

Becoming Prime Minister

IN 1990, FOLLOWING the fall of V.P. Singh's government, Chandra Shekhar was chosen to lead a minority government with the support of the Congress Party, which provided outside support without formally joining the government. On November 10, 1990, he was sworn in as the 8th Prime Minister of India.

Chandra Shekhar's government was characterized by its fragile nature, as it lacked a majority in the Lok Sabha, India's lower house of Parliament. This instability made it difficult for him to implement significant policies or reforms. However, he remained committed to maintaining the country's stability during a period of economic crisis and political uncertainty.

Economic Challenges

CHANDRA SHEKHAR'S TENURE as Prime Minister coincided with one of the most severe economic crises in India's post-independence history. The country faced a balance of payments crisis, with foreign exchange reserves dwindling to dangerously low levels. India was on the brink of defaulting on its international debt obligations, and the government was forced to mortgage gold reserves to secure emergency loans from the International Monetary Fund (IMF).

Despite these challenges, Chandra Shekhar's government took several important steps to stabilize the economy, including initiating discussions with the IMF for a bailout package. These efforts laid the groundwork for the economic reforms that would be implemented by the subsequent government of P.V. Narasimha Rao, which ultimately transformed India's economy.

Political Instability and Resignation

CHANDRA SHEKHAR'S GOVERNMENT was short-lived due to the lack of a stable majority and the withdrawal of support by the Congress Party, led by Rajiv Gandhi. The final blow came when Congress accused the government of spying on Rajiv Gandhi, leading to a political scandal that further eroded trust between the two parties.

On March 6, 1991, Chandra Shekhar resigned as Prime Minister, just eight months after taking office. However, he remained in a caretaker role until June 21, 1991, when new elections were held, and P.V. Narasimha Rao took over as Prime Minister.

Later Life and Legacy

AFTER RESIGNING AS Prime Minister, Chandra Shekhar continued to be an active figure in Indian politics, though he never held office again. He was respected across the political spectrum for his integrity, simplicity, and commitment to the principles of socialism and social justice. Chandra Shekhar was often referred to as the "People's Leader" because of his close connection with the common people and his deep understanding of their issues.

Chandra Shekhar passed away on July 8, 2007, after a prolonged illness. His legacy is that of a principled leader who stood by his beliefs, even when it meant challenging the political establishment. His tenure as Prime Minister, though brief, was marked by his efforts to navigate India through a period of significant economic and political challenges, earning him a place in the annals of Indian political history as a leader who valued integrity and social justice above all.

Chapter 11

P. V. Narasimha Rao (1991–1996)

PAMULAPARTI VENKATA Narasimha Rao, commonly known as P. V. Narasimha Rao, served as the Prime Minister of India from June 1991 to May 1996. Often hailed as the "Father of Indian Economic Reforms," his tenure was transformative, ushering in significant changes that reshaped the Indian economy and positioned India on the global stage. Rao's leadership during one of India's most challenging economic periods was marked by pragmatism, vision, and a willingness to take bold decisions.

Early Life and Education

P. V. NARASIMHA RAO was born on June 28, 1921, in Laknepalli village, in the Karimnagar district of what is now Telangana. He came from a middle-class agrarian family, which instilled in him a deep understanding of rural India's issues. Rao was an exceptional student, fluent in several languages, including Telugu, Marathi, Hindi, Sanskrit, Tamil, Urdu, French, and English. He pursued his higher education at the Osmania University in Hyderabad and later earned a law degree from the prestigious Hislop College in Nagpur.

Rao was deeply influenced by the Indian freedom struggle and joined the Indian National Congress during his student days. His involvement in the Quit India Movement in 1942 and his subsequent imprisonment by British authorities marked the beginning of his long and distinguished political career.

Political Career Before Becoming Prime Minister

P. V. NARASIMHA RAO'S political career began in the post-independence period when he was elected to the Andhra Pradesh Legislative Assembly. He served as a minister in the Andhra Pradesh government in various capacities, handling portfolios such as law and information, and eventually became the Chief Minister of Andhra Pradesh from 1971 to 1973. His tenure as Chief Minister was noted for his efforts to implement land reforms and improve education in the state.

In 1972, Rao was elected to the Lok Sabha, marking his entry into national politics. Over the years, he held several key portfolios in the Indian government, including Minister of External Affairs, Defense, Home Affairs, and Human Resource Development. Rao's reputation as a capable and efficient administrator grew during these years, and he became known for his deep knowledge of foreign affairs, his linguistic skills, and his ability to handle complex issues with a calm demeanor.

Becoming Prime Minister

THE ASSASSINATION OF Rajiv Gandhi in 1991 left the Congress Party in turmoil, with no clear leader to guide it through the upcoming elections. Despite his earlier decision to retire from active politics, P. V. Narasimha Rao was persuaded to return and lead the party. After the Congress Party emerged as the largest single party in the 1991 general elections, Rao was chosen as the Prime Minister, becoming the first person from South India to hold the office.

Economic Reforms and Liberalization

RAO'S TENURE AS PRIME Minister is most remembered for the sweeping economic reforms that he introduced, which fundamentally altered the trajectory of the Indian economy. When Rao took office, India was facing a severe balance of payments crisis, with foreign exchange reserves dwindling to perilous levels. The country was on the brink of default, and drastic measures were needed to stabilize the economy.

Recognizing the need for change, Rao appointed Dr. Manmohan Singh, a respected economist, as his Finance Minister. Together, they initiated a series of reforms aimed at liberalizing the Indian economy, which had been tightly controlled by the government since independence. These reforms included de-licensing industries, reducing import tariffs, promoting foreign investment, and dismantling the "License Raj" that had stifled economic growth.

The reforms marked a decisive shift from India's socialist-oriented economic policies to a more market-oriented approach. These changes, though initially met with resistance from various quarters, eventually led to a significant increase in foreign investment, a boost in industrial growth, and the integration of India into the global economy.

Foreign Policy Achievements

IN ADDITION TO HIS economic reforms, Rao also made significant contributions to India's foreign policy. He pursued a pragmatic and balanced approach, strengthening India's relations with key global powers, including the United States, Russia, and China. Rao's tenure saw the normalization of relations with Israel, with India establishing full diplomatic ties with the country in 1992.

Rao also played a crucial role in India's response to the changing global dynamics following the end of the Cold War. He recognized the importance of engaging with the emerging economies of Southeast Asia and launched the "Look East" policy, which aimed at enhancing economic and strategic ties with the countries of the region. This policy laid the foundation for India's increased engagement with Asia in the subsequent decades.

Political Challenges and Scandals

DESPITE HIS SUCCESSES, Rao's tenure was not without challenges. His government faced criticism for its handling of the Babri Masjid demolition in December 1992, which led to widespread communal violence across the country. The incident remains one of the most controversial and tragic events in India's post-independence history, and Rao's inability to prevent the demolition was widely condemned.

Rao's government was also plagued by several corruption scandals, including the infamous "JMM bribery case," in which members of Parliament were allegedly bribed to support the government in a no-confidence motion. Although Rao was later acquitted in this case, the allegations tarnished his reputation and weakened his political standing.

Later Life and Legacy

AFTER SERVING AS PRIME Minister, P. V. Narasimha Rao continued to be an influential figure in Indian politics, although his later years were marked by declining health and political isolation. He chose not to contest the 1996 elections, and the Congress Party's defeat in those elections marked the end of his active political career.

Rao spent his later years writing and reflecting on his time in office. He authored several books, including "The Insider," a semi-autobiographical novel that provided insights into the inner workings of Indian politics.

P. V. Narasimha Rao passed away on December 23, 2004, at the age of 83. His death marked the end of an era in Indian politics, but his legacy endures. Rao is remembered as a visionary leader who had the courage to implement bold economic reforms that transformed India into one of the world's fastest-growing economies. His tenure as Prime Minister was a turning point in India's history, and his contributions continue to shape the country's economic and foreign policy to this day.

Despite the controversies and challenges he faced, Rao's role in ushering in economic liberalization and his strategic vision for India's future have earned him a place among the most significant leaders in Indian history.

ATAL BIHARI VAJPAYEE, one of India's most revered political leaders, served as the Prime Minister of India in 1996 for a brief period of just 13 days. Although his first tenure as Prime Minister was short-lived, it marked the beginning of a significant shift in Indian politics, symbolizing the rise of the Bharatiya Janata Party (BJP) as a major national force. Vajpayee's charismatic leadership and his reputation as a moderate and statesmanlike figure played a crucial role in shaping the BJP's identity and expanding its appeal across the country.

Early Life and Education

ATAL BIHARI VAJPAYEE was born on December 25, 1924, in Gwalior, Madhya Pradesh, into a family with a strong educational background. His father, Krishna Bihari Vajpayee, was a poet and school teacher, which influenced young Atal's love for literature and poetry. Vajpayee pursued his education in Gwalior and later attended Victoria College (now Laxmi Bai College) in Gwalior, where he earned a degree in Hindi, English, and Sanskrit. He continued his education at DAV College, Kanpur, where he completed his post-graduation in Political Science.

Vajpayee was deeply influenced by the nationalist movement during his student days and became an active member of the Rashtriya Swayamsevak Sangh (RSS), a Hindu nationalist organization. His involvement with the RSS laid the foundation for his lifelong association with the ideology of Hindutva and his political career within the broader Sangh Parivar.

Political Beginnings

VAJPAYEE'S ENTRY INTO active politics began in the 1940s when he joined the Bharatiya Jana Sangh (BJS), the political arm of the RSS, founded by Dr. Syama Prasad Mookerjee. His oratory skills and ability to articulate the party's ideology in a way that resonated with the masses quickly made him a prominent figure within the BJS. He was elected to the Lok Sabha, the lower house of India's Parliament, for the first time in 1957 from Balrampur, Uttar Pradesh.

Throughout the 1960s and 1970s, Vajpayee played a key role in shaping the BJS's policies and strategies, advocating for a strong, unified India based on cultural nationalism. His speeches in Parliament were marked by a rare blend of wit, wisdom, and conviction, earning him respect across party lines.

Formation of the Bharatiya Janata Party

IN 1980, FOLLOWING the dissolution of the Janata Party, which had briefly united various opposition factions including the BJS, Vajpayee was instrumental in founding the Bharatiya Janata Party (BJP). The BJP was formed as the successor to the BJS, with a commitment to promoting Hindutva, economic nationalism, and a strong national defense.

Vajpayee became the BJP's first president and played a crucial role in expanding the party's base, making it a formidable political force. Under his leadership, the BJP focused on issues such as the Ram Janmabhoomi movement, which sought the construction of a temple at the disputed site in Ayodhya, and economic self-reliance.

1996 General Elections and Prime Ministership

THE 1996 GENERAL ELECTIONS were a turning point in Indian politics. The Congress Party, which had dominated Indian politics since independence, faced significant challenges, and the BJP emerged as the single largest party in the Lok Sabha with 161 seats. However, it was still short of a majority, leading to a situation where no party had a clear mandate to form the government.

On May 16, 1996, Atal Bihari Vajpayee was invited by the then-President of India, Dr. Shankar Dayal Sharma, to form the government. Vajpayee was sworn in as the 10th Prime Minister of India, marking the first time that a non-Congress leader from the BJP had ascended to the nation's highest office.

Challenges and Resignation

VAJPAYEE'S GOVERNMENT faced an immediate and formidable challenge: securing the necessary majority in the Lok Sabha. Despite his efforts to gather support from other parties, the BJP was unable to muster the required numbers. Vajpayee, known for his integrity and adherence to democratic principles, refused to indulge in unethical practices to win over members of Parliament.

Recognizing the impossibility of sustaining a government without a majority, Vajpayee chose to resign rather than face a vote of confidence that his government was certain to lose. On May 28, 1996, after just 13 days in office, Vajpayee submitted his resignation, paving the way for the formation of a United Front government supported by the Congress Party.

Legacy of the 1996 Tenure

ALTHOUGH VAJPAYEE'S first tenure as Prime Minister lasted only 13 days, it had a profound impact on Indian politics. His brief stint underscored the rise of the BJP as a credible alternative to the Congress Party, signaling a shift in the political landscape. Vajpayee's dignified and principled approach during this period earned him widespread respect and enhanced his stature as a national leader.

Vajpayee's short-lived government also set the stage for his later tenures as Prime Minister, during which he would go on to leave a lasting legacy. His leadership style, characterized by moderation, inclusivity, and a focus on national interest, helped the BJP gain broader acceptance among the Indian electorate.

Later Tenures and Lasting Impact

ATAL BIHARI VAJPAYEE would return as Prime Minister in 1998 and again in 1999, leading a coalition government that successfully completed a full term in office. His subsequent terms were marked by significant achievements, including India's nuclear tests in 1998, efforts to improve relations with Pakistan, and major economic reforms.

Vajpayee's legacy as a statesman, poet, and visionary leader remains a significant chapter in India's political history. His brief tenure in 1996, though short, was a prelude to a period of substantial change and development in the country, with Vajpayee at the helm of some of its most transformative years.

Chapter 13

H. D. Deve Gowda (1996–1997)

HARADANAHALLI DODDEGOWDA Deve Gowda, often known as H. D. Deve Gowda, served as the 11th Prime Minister of India from June 1996 to April 1997. His tenure as Prime Minister was relatively short and came at a time of considerable political instability in India. Despite the brevity of his time in office, Deve Gowda's leadership highlighted the growing importance of regional parties in Indian politics and the complexities of coalition governments.

Early Life and Education

H. D. DEVE GOWDA WAS born on May 18, 1933, in Haradanahalli, a small village in the Hassan district of Karnataka. He was born into a Vokkaliga family, an influential agrarian community in the region. Growing up in rural Karnataka, Deve Gowda was deeply connected to the land and the struggles of farmers, which would later influence his political ideology and career.

Deve Gowda completed his early education in his village and later graduated with a diploma in civil engineering from L. V. Polytechnic in Hassan. His background in engineering, combined with his agrarian roots, gave him a unique perspective on issues related to rural development, infrastructure, and agriculture.

Entry into Politics

DEVE GOWDA'S POLITICAL journey began in the 1950s when he became actively involved in local politics in Karnataka. He joined the Indian National Congress (INC) in 1953 and was elected to the Karnataka Legislative Assembly for the first time in 1962. Over the years, he became known for his work on behalf of farmers and his advocacy for rural development, which earned him a strong support base in his home state.

Deve Gowda's political career took a significant turn in 1967 when he left the Congress Party due to ideological differences and joined the Congress (O), a breakaway faction led by former Prime Minister Morarji Desai. Later, he became associated with the Janata Party, which emerged as a major force in Indian politics in the late 1970s, particularly after the Emergency imposed by Prime Minister Indira Gandhi.

Rise in Karnataka Politics

THROUGHOUT THE 1970S and 1980s, Deve Gowda continued to build his political career in Karnataka. He served as the Leader of the Opposition in the Karnataka Legislative Assembly from 1972 to 1976 and again from 1978 to 1983. His leadership during this period was marked by his focus on issues affecting rural communities, especially farmers, and his opposition to policies that he believed were detrimental to the agrarian sector.

In 1983, Deve Gowda became the Minister of Public Works and Irrigation in the Ramakrishna Hegde-led Janata Party government in Karnataka. His tenure as a minister was noted for his efforts to improve the state's irrigation infrastructure and his advocacy for the welfare of farmers. Deve Gowda's work in this area further solidified his reputation as a leader deeply committed to rural development.

Chief Minister of Karnataka

DEVE GOWDA'S POLITICAL career reached a new height in 1994 when he was elected as the Chief Minister of Karnataka. As Chief Minister, he focused on a range of issues, including irrigation, rural development, and infrastructure improvement. His government launched several initiatives aimed at improving the lives of farmers and the rural poor, reflecting his long-standing commitment to these issues.

During his tenure as Chief Minister, Deve Gowda also took steps to strengthen the state's economy by promoting industrial development and attracting investment. However, his government faced challenges, including opposition from within his party and from other political groups in the state. Despite these challenges, Deve Gowda's leadership as Chief Minister helped him gain prominence on the national stage.

Prime Minister of India

THE 1996 GENERAL ELECTIONS in India resulted in a hung Parliament, with no party winning a clear majority. The Bharatiya Janata Party (BJP) emerged as the single largest party but was unable to secure enough support to form a government. In this politically fragmented scenario, the United Front, a coalition of regional and left-leaning parties, came together to form a government with the support of the Congress Party.

After several rounds of negotiations, H. D. Deve Gowda, who was then the leader of the Janata Dal and a key figure in the United Front, was chosen as the consensus candidate for the Prime Ministership. On June 1, 1996, Deve Gowda was sworn in as the 11th Prime Minister of India.

Challenges of Coalition Politics

DEVE GOWDA'S TENURE as Prime Minister was marked by the challenges of managing a diverse coalition of regional parties with varying interests and priorities. As the head of a coalition government, Deve Gowda had to navigate the complexities of coalition politics, balancing the demands of different parties while trying to maintain a stable government.

Despite these challenges, Deve Gowda's government initiated several important policies, particularly in the areas of rural development and infrastructure. His administration continued to focus on the issues close to his heart, such as agriculture and irrigation, and he sought to address the needs of India's vast rural population.

However, the coalition's internal contradictions and the lack of cohesive support from the Congress Party, which was providing external support to the government, made it difficult for Deve Gowda to implement his full agenda. The constant threat of losing the Congress Party's support created an atmosphere of uncertainty and limited the government's effectiveness.

End of Tenure

DEVE GOWDA'S TENURE as Prime Minister came to an abrupt end in April 1997 when the Congress Party withdrew its support from the United Front government. The decision was influenced by various factors, including dissatisfaction with Deve Gowda's leadership and internal party dynamics within the Congress. Unable to secure a vote of confidence in the Lok Sabha, Deve Gowda resigned as Prime Minister on April 11, 1997, after serving for just under 11 months.

Following his resignation, I. K. Gujral, another senior leader of the United Front, was chosen to succeed Deve Gowda as Prime Minister. Despite the brevity of his tenure, Deve Gowda's time as Prime Minister highlighted the increasing influence of regional parties in Indian politics and the challenges of coalition governance in a diverse and complex democracy like India.

Later Life and Legacy

AFTER STEPPING DOWN as Prime Minister, H. D. Deve Gowda continued to be an influential figure in Indian politics, particularly in Karnataka. He remained active in the Janata Dal (Secular), a faction of the original Janata Dal, and played a key role in Karnataka's state politics.

Deve Gowda's political career has been marked by his deep commitment to the welfare of farmers and rural communities, a legacy that continues to define his public image. His brief tenure as Prime Minister is remembered as a period of political experimentation, reflecting the evolving nature of India's democracy and the growing importance of regional leaders on the national stage.

Despite the challenges and limitations of his time in office, Deve Gowda's leadership as Prime Minister demonstrated the potential of coalition governments to bring together diverse political forces in pursuit of common goals. His contributions to Indian politics, particularly in the areas of rural development and coalition governance, continue to be recognized and respected.

Chapter 14:
I. K. Gujral (1997–1998)

INDER KUMAR GUJRAL, commonly known as I. K. Gujral, served as the 12th Prime Minister of India from April 1997 to March 1998. His tenure, though brief, was marked by a focus on foreign policy and efforts to maintain stability in a complex coalition government. Gujral was known for his diplomatic acumen and his emphasis on maintaining peaceful and cooperative relations with India's neighbors, an approach that later came to be known as the "Gujral Doctrine."

Early Life and Education

I. K. GUJRAL WAS BORN on December 4, 1919, in Jhelum, a town in present-day Pakistan, which was then part of British India. He was born into a well-educated and politically active family. His father, Avtar Narain Gujral, was a prominent social worker and politician, and his mother, Pushpa Gujral, was a freedom fighter who participated in the Quit India Movement.

Gujral grew up in an environment that nurtured his intellectual and political development. He completed his early education in Jhelum and later attended DAV College, Hailey College of Commerce, and Forman Christian College in Lahore. He was actively involved in the student movement against British rule and participated in various activities organized by the Indian National Congress.

Political Career and Diplomatic Service

AFTER THE PARTITION of India in 1947, Gujral and his family moved to New Delhi. He soon became involved in politics and joined the Indian National Congress. Gujral's political career began in earnest when he was elected to the Rajya Sabha, the upper house of India's Parliament, in 1964. He quickly established himself as a capable and articulate politician, known for his intellectual approach to issues.

Gujral's diplomatic skills were recognized early in his career, leading to his appointment as India's Ambassador to the Soviet Union in 1976, during the height of the Cold War. His tenure as Ambassador was marked by efforts to strengthen Indo-Soviet relations, a key aspect of India's foreign policy at the time. His experience in diplomacy and his deep understanding of international affairs would later play a significant role in shaping his approach as Prime Minister.

Return to Politics and the Janata Dal

AFTER HIS STINT AS Ambassador, Gujral returned to active politics and joined the Janata Dal, a party formed by the merger of several opposition groups following the Emergency imposed by Prime Minister Indira Gandhi. He held various ministerial positions in successive governments, including Minister of Information and Broadcasting and Minister of External Affairs.

As Minister of External Affairs under Prime Minister V. P. Singh in 1989, Gujral played a crucial role in shaping India's foreign policy. His tenure was marked by efforts to strengthen India's ties with neighboring countries and to enhance India's role in international organizations. Gujral's commitment to peace and regional cooperation became a hallmark of his approach to diplomacy.

Becoming Prime Minister

THE POLITICAL LANDSCAPE in India during the mid-1990s was characterized by fragmentation and instability. The United Front, a coalition of regional and left-leaning parties, had come to power with the support of the Congress Party after the 1996 general elections. However, internal differences and the withdrawal of Congress support led to the resignation of Prime Minister H. D. Deve Gowda in April 1997.

Following Deve Gowda's resignation, I. K. Gujral was chosen as the consensus candidate to lead the United Front government. He was sworn in as the 12th Prime Minister of India on April 21, 1997. Gujral's appointment as Prime Minister was seen as a move to stabilize the government and ensure continuity, given his reputation as a seasoned diplomat and a moderate leader.

The Gujral Doctrine

ONE OF THE MOST SIGNIFICANT aspects of Gujral's tenure as Prime Minister was his approach to foreign policy, which came to be known as the "Gujral Doctrine." This doctrine emphasized the importance of maintaining good relations with India's neighbors, particularly the smaller countries in South Asia. Gujral advocated for a policy of non-reciprocity, where India would not demand anything in return for its assistance to its neighbors, thereby fostering goodwill and cooperation.

The Gujral Doctrine aimed to build trust and resolve conflicts through dialogue and mutual respect. It reflected Gujral's belief that India's security and prosperity were closely linked to the stability and development of the entire South Asian region. This approach led to improved relations with several neighboring countries, including Bangladesh, Nepal, and Sri Lanka, and helped to ease tensions in a region often marked by rivalry and conflict.

Domestic Challenges and Coalition Politics

GUJRAL'S TENURE AS Prime Minister was marked by the challenges of managing a diverse and often fractious coalition. The United Front government comprised several regional parties with differing agendas, making it difficult to maintain unity and coherence. Gujral's leadership style, which emphasized consensus and dialogue, helped to some extent in managing these differences, but the inherent instability of the coalition remained a constant challenge.

The biggest challenge to Gujral's government came in late 1997, when the Congress Party, led by Sitaram Kesri, withdrew its support over differences related to the investigation of the Jain Commission report. The report had implicated members of the Dravida Munnetra Kazhagam (DMK), a key ally of the United Front, in the assassination of former Prime Minister Rajiv Gandhi. The withdrawal of Congress support led to the collapse of the United Front government.

End of Tenure and Later Life

I. K. GUJRAL RESIGNED as Prime Minister on March 19, 1998, after the Congress Party's withdrawal of support made it impossible for his government to continue. The fall of the United Front government led to fresh elections, and Gujral's tenure as Prime Minister came to an end after less than a year in office.

After stepping down as Prime Minister, Gujral continued to be an influential voice in Indian politics and international affairs. He remained active in public life, contributing to discussions on foreign policy, governance, and regional cooperation. Gujral's legacy as a statesman and diplomat is particularly remembered for his emphasis on peace and cooperation in South Asia, as well as his efforts to maintain stability during a turbulent period in Indian politics.

I. K. Gujral passed away on November 30, 2012, at the age of 92. His contributions to Indian politics and diplomacy continue to be recognized and respected, particularly his efforts to promote regional harmony and his vision of a peaceful and prosperous South Asia.

Chapter 15:
Atal Bihari Vajpayee (1998–2004)

ATAL BIHARI VAJPAYEE, one of India's most respected and influential leaders, served as the 10th Prime Minister of India in three terms—first for a brief period in 1996, then from 1998 to 2004. His tenure as Prime Minister is widely remembered for his efforts to strengthen India's economy, improve its infrastructure, and enhance its standing on the global stage. Vajpayee's leadership was marked by his ability to build consensus, his commitment to national integration, and his vision for a strong and prosperous India.

Early Life and Education

ATAL BIHARI VAJPAYEE was born on December 25, 1924, in Gwalior, in present-day Madhya Pradesh. He was born into a middle-class Brahmin family, with his father, Krishna Bihari Vajpayee, being a school teacher and a poet. Vajpayee inherited his father's love for poetry, which became a lifelong passion.

Vajpayee completed his schooling in Gwalior and later attended Laxmi Bai College, where he studied Hindi, English, and Sanskrit. He went on to complete his post-graduation in Political Science from Victoria College (now known as Maharani Laxmi Bai Government College of Excellence) in Gwalior. He further pursued law at DAV College in Kanpur but did not complete his degree, as his interest in politics grew stronger.

Entry into Politics

VAJPAYEE'S POLITICAL career began in the early 1940s when he joined the Rashtriya Swayamsevak Sangh (RSS), a Hindu nationalist organization. His involvement with the RSS played a crucial role in shaping his political ideology, which was centered around the promotion of Indian culture and values. He was also an active participant in the Indian freedom movement and was briefly imprisoned during the Quit India Movement in 1942.

In 1951, Vajpayee joined the newly formed Bharatiya Jana Sangh (BJS), the political wing of the RSS. He quickly rose through the ranks, becoming a prominent leader within the party. Vajpayee was elected to the Lok Sabha, the lower house of India's Parliament, for the first time in 1957 from Balrampur, Uttar Pradesh. His eloquence and oratory skills made him a respected voice in Parliament, and he soon became one of the key leaders of the BJS.

Rise in National Politics

THROUGHOUT THE 1960S and 1970s, Vajpayee continued to build his political career, serving as the President of the Bharatiya Jana Sangh from 1968 to 1973. He was a staunch critic of the Congress Party and its policies, particularly during the Emergency imposed by Prime Minister Indira Gandhi in 1975. During the Emergency, Vajpayee, along with several other opposition leaders, was arrested and detained.

In 1977, following the lifting of the Emergency, Vajpayee played a significant role in the formation of the Janata Party, a coalition of opposition parties that came together to challenge the Congress Party. The Janata Party won a historic victory in the 1977 general elections, and Vajpayee was appointed as the Minister of External Affairs in Prime Minister Morarji Desai's government. As Foreign Minister, Vajpayee made a mark with his efforts to improve India's relations with its neighbors and other countries.

Formation of the Bharatiya Janata Party

IN 1980, FOLLOWING internal conflicts within the Janata Party, Vajpayee and his colleagues from the Bharatiya Jana Sangh decided to form a new party, the Bharatiya Janata Party (BJP). Vajpayee was appointed as the party's first President. Under his leadership, the BJP sought to establish itself as a major national party with a platform that emphasized cultural nationalism, economic development, and strong governance.

Throughout the 1980s and early 1990s, Vajpayee continued to be a prominent figure in Indian politics, although the BJP remained in the opposition. However, the political landscape in India began to change in the 1990s, with the BJP gaining significant support across the country, particularly after the Ram Janmabhoomi movement, which advocated for the construction of a temple at the disputed site in Ayodhya.

First Term as Prime Minister

IN THE 1996 GENERAL elections, the BJP emerged as the single largest party in the Lok Sabha, and Vajpayee was invited to form the government. On May 16, 1996, he was sworn in as the Prime Minister of India for the first time. However, due to a lack of a majority in Parliament, Vajpayee's government lasted only 13 days, and he resigned before a vote of confidence could be held.

Second and Third Terms as Prime Minister

VAJPAYEE'S SECOND TERM as Prime Minister began on March 19, 1998, after the BJP-led National Democratic Alliance (NDA) secured a majority in the general elections. This term marked a significant period in India's history, as Vajpayee's government undertook several important initiatives in both domestic and foreign policy.

One of the most notable events during Vajpayee's tenure was the successful conduct of nuclear tests in Pokhran, Rajasthan, in May 1998. These tests established India as a nuclear-armed state, leading to international sanctions but also earning India respect as a global power. Vajpayee's government handled the international fallout with diplomatic skill, and within a few years, most of the sanctions were lifted.

Vajpayee's government also focused on economic reforms, infrastructure development, and social welfare programs. Under his leadership, India experienced significant economic growth, and initiatives such as the Golden Quadrilateral project, which aimed to improve the country's road network, were launched. Vajpayee also introduced the Sarva Shiksha Abhiyan, a program aimed at universalizing elementary education in India.

In terms of foreign policy, Vajpayee sought to improve India's relations with its neighbors, particularly Pakistan. In February 1999, he undertook a historic bus journey to Lahore, where he signed the

Lahore Declaration with Pakistani Prime Minister Nawaz Sharif, committing both countries to resolving their differences through dialogue. However, relations with Pakistan soured later that year due to the Kargil War, in which the Indian military successfully repelled an infiltration by Pakistani forces in the Kargil region of Jammu and Kashmir.

Third Term and Challenges

VAJPAYEE'S THIRD TERM as Prime Minister began after the 1999 general elections, in which the BJP-led NDA secured a decisive victory. This term saw continued economic reforms and efforts to strengthen India's infrastructure. However, Vajpayee's government also faced significant challenges, including communal tensions, particularly following the 2002 Gujarat riots, and the threat of terrorism.

Despite these challenges, Vajpayee's leadership was marked by his ability to maintain stability and promote economic growth. He was known for his moderate approach, his emphasis on consensus-building, and his vision for a united and prosperous India.

Retirement and Legacy

ATAL BIHARI VAJPAYEE'S tenure as Prime Minister came to an end in May 2004, when the NDA was unexpectedly defeated in the general elections by the Congress-led United Progressive Alliance (UPA). Following the elections, Vajpayee stepped down from active politics, citing health reasons.

Vajpayee's legacy as Prime Minister is remembered for his contributions to India's economic development, his efforts to improve relations with neighboring countries, and his commitment to democratic values and governance. He was a poet at heart, and his speeches and writings continue to inspire generations of Indians.

In 2014, Vajpayee was awarded the Bharat Ratna, India's highest civilian honor, in recognition of his services to the nation. He passed away on August 16, 2018, at the age of 93. His legacy as a statesman, a visionary leader, and a unifying figure in Indian politics endures to this day.

Chapter 16

Dr. Manmohan Singh (2004–2014)

DR. MANMOHAN SINGH served as the 13th Prime Minister of India from 2004 to 2014, becoming the first Sikh to hold the office. Known for his economic expertise, humility, and integrity, Singh played a pivotal role in shaping modern India's economic policies, both as Finance Minister in the early 1990s and as Prime Minister in the 2000s. His tenure as Prime Minister is marked by significant economic growth, social welfare schemes, and efforts to strengthen India's position on the global stage.

Early Life and Education

MANMOHAN SINGH WAS born on September 26, 1932, in Gah, a small village in the Punjab province of British India, now in Pakistan. His early life was marked by the upheaval of the Partition in 1947, which forced his family to migrate to Amritsar in India. Despite these challenges, Singh excelled academically from a young age.

Singh pursued his undergraduate studies at Government College in Lahore before moving to India after Partition. He later attended Panjab University in Chandigarh, where he earned his bachelor's and master's degrees in Economics. His academic brilliance earned him a scholarship to study at the University of Cambridge, where he completed his second undergraduate degree, followed by a DPhil in Economics from the University of Oxford. His doctoral thesis, "India's Export Trends and Prospects for Self-Sustained Growth," would later influence India's economic policies.

Academic and Professional Career

BEFORE ENTERING POLITICS, Dr. Singh had a distinguished academic and bureaucratic career. He held various positions in academia, including as a professor at the Delhi School of Economics and the Punjab University. He also worked with several international organizations, including the United Nations Conference on Trade and Development (UNCTAD), and served as an advisor to the Ministry of Foreign Trade.

Dr. Singh's expertise in economics led to his appointment as the Chief Economic Advisor in the Ministry of Finance in 1972, and later as the Governor of the Reserve Bank of India from 1982 to 1985. He also served as the Deputy Chairman of the Planning Commission, where he played a crucial role in formulating India's economic policies during the 1980s.

Architect of Economic Reforms

DR. SINGH'S ENTRY INTO active politics came in 1991, when Prime Minister P. V. Narasimha Rao appointed him as the Finance Minister of India. At that time, India was facing a severe economic crisis, with dwindling foreign exchange reserves and a looming balance of payments crisis. Dr. Singh was tasked with rescuing the Indian economy from the brink of collapse.

As Finance Minister, Dr. Singh implemented a series of landmark economic reforms that liberalized the Indian economy. These reforms included reducing government control over industries, opening up the economy to foreign investments, and introducing fiscal discipline. His policies marked the beginning of India's transition from a state-controlled economy to a market-driven one. The reforms laid the foundation for the economic growth that India experienced in the following decades, earning Dr. Singh widespread acclaim both domestically and internationally.

Becoming Prime Minister

AFTER THE CONGRESS Party's unexpected victory in the 2004 general elections, Sonia Gandhi, the party's leader, chose Dr. Manmohan Singh to be the Prime Minister of India. His appointment was seen as a move to ensure economic stability and continuity of the reform process initiated in the early 1990s. Dr. Singh was sworn in as Prime Minister on May 22, 2004.

First Term as Prime Minister (2004–2009)

DR. SINGH'S FIRST TERM as Prime Minister was characterized by robust economic growth, with India's GDP growing at an average rate of over 8% per year. His government implemented several key social welfare programs, including the Mahatma Gandhi National Rural Employment Guarantee Act (MGNREGA), which aimed to provide job security to rural households, and the Right to Information Act (RTI), which enhanced transparency and accountability in government.

On the international front, Dr. Singh played a significant role in improving India's relations with major global powers. One of his most notable achievements was the signing of the India–United States Civil Nuclear Agreement in 2008, which ended India's nuclear isolation and allowed it to access civilian nuclear technology from other countries. This agreement was a cornerstone of India's foreign policy under Dr. Singh, as it marked a significant shift in India-U.S. relations.

However, his first term also faced challenges, particularly from within the coalition government he led. The government had to navigate opposition from left-wing parties on economic policies and faced criticism over its handling of issues like inflation and agrarian distress.

Second Term as Prime Minister

(2009–2014)

THE CONGRESS-LED UNITED Progressive Alliance (UPA) won the 2009 general elections, and Dr. Singh was re-elected as Prime Minister. His second term began with high hopes, as the UPA had secured a larger majority, allowing for more stability and potential for further reforms.

During his second term, Dr. Singh continued to focus on economic growth and social welfare. His government launched the National Food Security Act, which aimed to provide subsidized food grains to two-thirds of India's population. The Right to Education Act, another significant achievement, was passed, making education a fundamental right for children aged 6 to 14 years.

However, Dr. Singh's second term was overshadowed by a series of high-profile corruption scandals, including the 2G spectrum scam and the Commonwealth Games scam. These scandals led to widespread public outrage and damaged the government's credibility. Despite his personal reputation for integrity, Dr. Singh was criticized for being unable to prevent corruption within his government and for what many perceived as a lack of decisive leadership in dealing with the scandals.

Challenges and Criticisms

WHILE DR. SINGH WAS widely respected for his intellect and integrity, his tenure as Prime Minister was not without challenges. Critics often labeled him as a "silent" Prime Minister, particularly during his second term, accusing him of not speaking out strongly enough against corruption or asserting his authority within the coalition government. The perception of a weak and indecisive leadership contributed to a decline in the Congress Party's popularity.

Another significant challenge during Dr. Singh's tenure was the global financial crisis of 2008, which impacted India's economy. Although India managed to recover relatively quickly compared to other countries, the crisis exposed vulnerabilities in the Indian economy, leading to concerns about inflation, fiscal deficits, and slowing growth in the latter part of his second term.

Legacy and Later Life

DR. MANMOHAN SINGH stepped down as Prime Minister after the Congress Party's defeat in the 2014 general elections, which brought Narendra Modi and the Bharatiya Janata Party (BJP) to power. After leaving office, Dr. Singh continued to be an influential figure in Indian politics and economics, offering his insights on various issues and serving as a senior leader of the Congress Party.

Dr. Singh's legacy is complex and multifaceted. He is widely regarded as the architect of India's economic liberalization and credited with steering the country through a period of rapid economic growth and development. His policies helped transform India into one of the world's fastest-growing major economies. However, his tenure as Prime Minister also saw significant challenges, particularly in his second term, where his government was marred by allegations of corruption and a perception of weak leadership.

Despite these challenges, Dr. Manmohan Singh remains a respected figure in Indian public life, known for his humility, intellect, and dedication to public service. His contributions to India's economic and political landscape continue to be recognized and studied by scholars and policymakers alike.

Chapter 17:
Narendra Modi (2014–Present)

NARENDRA MODI, THE 14th and current Prime Minister of India, has been a transformative figure in Indian politics since taking office in 2014. Known for his charismatic leadership, decisive governance, and ambitious vision for India, Modi's tenure has seen significant changes in the country's political, economic, and social landscape. His leadership style, policies, and impact have made him one of the most influential leaders in modern Indian history.

Early Life and Education

NARENDRA DAMODARDAS Modi was born on September 17, 1950, in Vadnagar, a small town in the Mehsana district of Gujarat. He was the third of six children born to Damodardas Mulchand Modi and Heeraben Modi. His family belonged to the Ghanchi-Teli community, a backward class that traditionally worked as oil-pressers. Despite the family's modest means, Modi's early life was marked by hard work and perseverance. As a young boy, he helped his father sell tea at the local railway station, a fact that would later become a significant part of his political persona.

Modi completed his schooling in Vadnagar, where he was known as an average student but a keen debater and an active participant in extracurricular activities. He had a deep interest in Hindu scriptures and Indian culture from an early age, which later influenced his political ideology. After completing high school, Modi left home and traveled across India for two years, visiting various ashrams and religious centers, which deepened his spiritual beliefs and understanding of the country.

Upon his return, Modi earned a degree in political science from the University of Delhi through distance education. He later obtained a Master's degree in political science from Gujarat University.

Entry into Politics

NARENDRA MODI'S POLITICAL journey began at an early age when he joined the Rashtriya Swayamsevak Sangh (RSS), a Hindu nationalist organization, in the 1970s. His involvement with the RSS played a crucial role in shaping his political career and ideology. As a pracharak (campaigner) of the RSS, Modi worked closely with grassroots organizations, gaining experience in organizational work and developing a deep understanding of Indian society.

In 1987, Modi joined the Bharatiya Janata Party (BJP), the political wing of the RSS. He quickly rose through the ranks due to his organizational skills and dedication. Modi played a key role in the BJP's campaign during the 1995 Gujarat state elections, which led to the party's victory and established his reputation as an effective strategist.

Chief Minister of Gujarat (2001–2014)

MODI'S POLITICAL CAREER took a significant turn in 2001 when he was appointed as the Chief Minister of Gujarat, following the resignation of Keshubhai Patel. His tenure as Chief Minister was marked by both achievements and controversies.

One of the most significant events during Modi's time as Chief Minister was the 2002 Gujarat riots, which erupted following the Godhra train burning incident. The violence resulted in the deaths of over 1,000 people, most of whom were Muslims. Modi's handling of the riots attracted widespread criticism, both in India and internationally, with accusations of state complicity and failure to prevent the violence. Despite these controversies, Modi was repeatedly elected as Chief Minister, serving in the position until 2014.

During his time as Chief Minister, Modi focused on economic development and infrastructure. His policies, known as the "Gujarat model," emphasized industrialization, investment in infrastructure, and improving the ease of doing business. Under his leadership, Gujarat experienced significant economic growth, attracting investments from both domestic and international businesses. Modi's success in Gujarat bolstered his image as a pro-business, development-oriented leader, which would later become central to his national political campaign.

Prime Minister of India (2014–Present)

NARENDRA MODI LED THE BJP to a decisive victory in the 2014 general elections, securing an absolute majority in the Lok Sabha, the first time a single party had done so since 1984. He was sworn in as the Prime Minister of India on May 26, 2014. Modi's rise to the premiership was seen as a shift in Indian politics, with a focus on strong leadership, economic development, and nationalism.

First Term (2014–2019)

MODI'S FIRST TERM AS Prime Minister was marked by several significant initiatives and reforms aimed at transforming India's economy and governance. Some of the key initiatives launched during this period include:

1. Make in India: Aimed at boosting manufacturing in India and attracting foreign investment, this initiative sought to transform India into a global manufacturing hub.

2. Digital India: Launched to improve online infrastructure, increase internet connectivity, and make government services more accessible to citizens electronically.

3. Swachh Bharat Abhiyan: A nationwide cleanliness campaign that aimed to eliminate open defecation and improve sanitation across India.

4. Goods and Services Tax (GST): Implemented in 2017, GST replaced a complex system of indirect taxes with a single, unified tax structure, making it one of the most significant tax reforms in Indian history.

5. Demonetization: In November 2016, Modi announced the sudden demonetization of ₹500 and ₹1,000 currency notes, a move aimed at curbing black money, counterfeit currency, and corruption. While the move was highly controversial and led to significant short-term economic disruption, it was also praised by some for its boldness.

6. Jan Dhan Yojana: A financial inclusion program aimed at ensuring that every household in India had access to a bank account.

On the foreign policy front, Modi sought to enhance India's global standing through active diplomacy and engagement with world leaders. He emphasized stronger ties with neighboring countries, the United States, and Japan, while also focusing on energy security and economic partnerships.

Second Term (2019–2024)

IN THE 2019 GENERAL elections, Modi led the BJP to an even larger victory, securing over 300 seats in the Lok Sabha. His second term has been characterized by continued focus on economic reforms, national security, and social welfare programs.

Key initiatives and events during Modi's second term include:

1. Abrogation of Article 370: In August 2019, the government revoked Article 370 of the Indian Constitution, which granted special status to Jammu and Kashmir. The move was highly controversial and led to significant political and security challenges in the region.

2. Citizenship Amendment Act (CAA): Passed in December 2019, the CAA provided a pathway to citizenship for non-Muslim refugees from neighboring countries. The Act led to widespread protests and criticism, with opponents arguing that it undermined India's secular character.

3. Atmanirbhar Bharat: Launched in response to the COVID-19 pandemic, this initiative aimed to make India

self-reliant by promoting local manufacturing, reducing dependence on imports, and encouraging innovation.

4. Farm Laws: In 2020, the Modi government introduced three agricultural reform laws aimed at liberalizing the farm sector. The laws led to massive protests by farmers, particularly in Punjab and Haryana, and were eventually repealed in November 2021.

5. COVID-19 Pandemic Management: Modi's government faced the unprecedented challenge of managing the COVID-19 pandemic. The administration implemented nationwide lockdowns, ramped up healthcare infrastructure, and launched one of the world's largest vaccination drives. While the initial response was praised, the second wave in 2021, marked by a severe shortage of medical supplies and oxygen, drew significant criticism.

6. National Education Policy 2020: This policy marked a significant overhaul of India's education system, with a focus on holistic development, flexibility in learning, and the integration of technology in education.

. . . .

Third Term (2024–Present)

AS OF 2024, NARENDRA Modi has embarked on his third term as the Prime Minister of India, following a historic victory in the general elections. This victory marks Modi's continued dominance in Indian politics, reinforcing his position as one of the most significant leaders in the country's post-independence history.

Election Victory and Mandate

THE 2024 GENERAL ELECTIONS were seen as a critical test of Modi's leadership after a decade in power. Despite challenges, including economic issues, social unrest, and criticism of his handling of certain policies, Modi and the Bharatiya Janata Party (BJP) secured a decisive mandate. The victory was attributed to Modi's strong personal appeal, effective campaigning, and the BJP's organizational strength. Key issues in the election included national security, economic growth, and social welfare programs.

Key Priorities and Initiatives

IN HIS THIRD TERM, Modi has emphasized continuity and expansion of his previous initiatives while addressing new challenges facing the nation. Some of the key priorities include:

1. Economic Revival: Modi's third term has been marked by a strong focus on reviving and strengthening the Indian economy. With global economic uncertainties and domestic challenges, the government has introduced policies aimed at boosting investment, enhancing infrastructure, and promoting job creation. The focus has been on accelerating growth in sectors like manufacturing, technology, and agriculture.

2. Social Welfare and Inclusive Development: Continuing his emphasis on social welfare, Modi has expanded programs aimed at improving the lives of marginalized communities. This includes enhancing access to healthcare, education, and financial services, particularly in rural areas. New initiatives have been launched to further improve sanitation, housing, and clean energy access, in line with the goals of sustainable development.

3. Digital and Technological Advancement: Building on the success of the Digital India initiative, Modi's third term has seen a push towards further digitalization and technological innovation. This includes efforts to integrate artificial intelligence, 5G technology, and digital infrastructure into the broader economy and governance. The government has also focused on fostering startups and innovation, with the aim of making India a global technology leader.

4. Environmental Sustainability: Recognizing the global emphasis on climate change, Modi has prioritized environmental sustainability in his third term. This includes commitments to reducing carbon emissions, promoting renewable energy, and implementing policies aimed at preserving biodiversity and water resources. The government has also been working on enhancing disaster preparedness and resilience in response to climate-related challenges.

5. Foreign Policy and Global Standing: Modi's third term has seen continued efforts to enhance India's global standing. This includes strengthening ties with key global powers, expanding trade relations, and playing a more active role in international organizations. Modi has also focused on regional security and stability, particularly in the context of tensions with neighboring countries and the broader Indo-Pacific region.

Challenges and Criticisms

DESPITE HIS ELECTORAL success, Modi's third term has not been without challenges. Economic issues, including inflation and unemployment, remain significant concerns. Social and political polarization continues to be a contentious issue, with critics arguing that certain policies have exacerbated divisions within Indian society. Additionally, the government's handling of foreign relations, particularly with China and Pakistan, has faced scrutiny.

Legacy and Future Prospects

AS MODI NAVIGATES HIS third term, his legacy continues to evolve. His impact on Indian politics, governance, and society is profound, with supporters praising his vision and decisive leadership, while critics highlight concerns about democratic institutions and social harmony. The third term will be crucial in defining Modi's long-term legacy, particularly in terms of economic recovery, social cohesion, and India's role on the global stage.

The success of Modi's third term will likely shape the future of Indian politics for years to come, with potential implications for the BJP's dominance and the broader political landscape of the country.

Internationally, Modi has positioned India as a key player on the global stage, forging stronger ties with major powers while asserting India's interests in regional and global affairs. His tenure has seen India take a more assertive stance on issues of national security, particularly with regard to Pakistan and China.

As of 2024, Narendra Modi remains one of the most influential and polarizing figures in Indian politics. His leadership has brought about significant changes in India's political, economic, and social landscape, and his legacy will be debated and studied for years to come. Whether admired for his vision and decisiveness or criticized for his polarizing policies, Modi's influence on India is undeniable.

Summary of all Chapter's

Part I: Presidents of India

1. Dr. Rajendra Prasad (1950–1962)

Summary: India's first President, Dr. Rajendra Prasad, served two terms and played a crucial role in shaping the newly independent nation. Known for his humility and dedication, he was instrumental in drafting the Indian Constitution and fostering unity in the diverse country.

2. Dr. Sarvepalli Radhakrishnan (1962–1967)

Summary: A renowned philosopher and statesman, Dr. Radhakrishnan was India's second President. His tenure was marked by efforts to promote education and uphold India's cultural values. He is remembered for his intellectual contributions and commitment to promoting peace.

3. Dr. Zakir Husain (1967–1969)

Summary: The first Muslim President of India, Dr. Zakir Husain, was an educationist and a strong advocate of secularism and national unity. His presidency was cut short by his sudden death, but his legacy as a promoter of education and cultural integration endures.

4. Varahagiri Venkata Giri (1969–1974)

Summary: V. V. Giri, initially an acting President, became the only President elected as an independent candidate. His presidency was marked by his support for labor rights and social justice, reflecting his background as a trade union leader.

5. Fakhruddin Ali Ahmed (1974–1977)

Summary: As the fifth President of India, Fakhruddin Ali Ahmed is best remembered for his controversial role during the Emergency imposed by then-Prime Minister Indira Gandhi. Despite the political turmoil, he remained committed to constitutional principles.

6. Neelam Sanjiva Reddy (1977–1982)

Summary: Neelam Sanjiva Reddy, the sixth President of India, was elected unopposed. His tenure was notable for its emphasis on parliamentary democracy and his efforts to maintain political neutrality and integrity during a time of political instability.

7. Giani Zail Singh (1982–1987)

Summary: Giani Zail Singh's tenure as President was marked by a strong commitment to social justice and secularism. However, his term also saw significant tensions with Prime Minister Indira Gandhi, particularly during Operation Blue Star.

8. R. Venkataraman (1987–1992)

Summary: A seasoned politician and economist, R. Venkataraman's presidency was characterized by his focus on economic development and his efforts to stabilize the Indian economy. He played a key role in guiding India through a challenging period of economic and political transition.

9. Dr. Shankar Dayal Sharma (1992–1997)

Summary: Dr. Shankar Dayal Sharma, known for his scholarly background, served as the ninth President of India. His presidency was marked by his emphasis on constitutional governance and upholding the dignity of the office during a time of political flux.

10. K. R. Narayanan (1997–2002)

Summary: K. R. Narayanan, India's first Dalit President, was known for his strong commitment to social justice and human rights. His presidency was notable for his proactive role in addressing social inequalities and advocating for the marginalized sections of society.

11. Dr. A. P. J. Abdul Kalam (2002–2007)

Summary: Popularly known as the "People's President," Dr. A. P. J. Abdul Kalam was a renowned scientist and visionary. His presidency inspired millions of Indians, particularly the youth, with his emphasis on education, innovation, and national development.

12. Pratibha Patil (2007–2012)

Summary: India's first female President, Pratibha Patil's tenure focused on women's empowerment, education, and social welfare. Despite facing criticism, she remains a symbol of progress in the representation of women in Indian politics.

13. Pranab Mukherjee (2012–2017)

Summary: A veteran politician with decades of experience, Pranab Mukherjee's presidency was marked by his efforts to uphold democratic values and constitutional principles. He played a crucial role in bridging gaps between the government and the opposition.

14. Ram Nath Kovind (2017–2022)

Summary: Ram Nath Kovind, India's second Dalit President, focused on promoting social harmony, education, and constitutional values. His presidency was notable for its quiet but firm emphasis on inclusivity and justice for all sections of society.

15. Droupadi Murmu (2022–Present)

Summary: As the first tribal President of India, Droupadi Murmu's presidency represents a significant step towards inclusivity and representation for marginalized communities. Her tenure is marked by her commitment to social justice, tribal rights, and environmental sustainability.

• • • •

Part II: Prime Ministers of India

1. JAWAHARLAL NEHRU (1947–1964)

Summary: India's first Prime Minister, Nehru laid the foundations for modern India with his vision of a secular, democratic, and socialist nation. His policies on industrialization, education, and foreign relations shaped the early years of independent India.

2. Gulzarilal Nanda (1964, Acting)

Summary: Nanda served as acting Prime Minister twice, during times of political transition. Though his tenure was brief, he is remembered for his commitment to stability and continuity in governance.

3. Lal Bahadur Shastri (1964–1966)

Summary: Shastri is best known for his slogan "Jai Jawan Jai Kisan" and his leadership during the 1965 Indo-Pakistan War. His tenure, though short, was marked by his focus on agricultural development and national security.

4. Gulzarilal Nanda (1966, Acting)

Summary: Once again, Nanda served as acting Prime Minister during a crucial transition period after Shastri's sudden death, ensuring a smooth handover of power to his successor.

5. Indira Gandhi (1966–1977)

Summary: Indira Gandhi, the first and only female Prime Minister of India, was a central figure in Indian politics for nearly two decades. Her tenure was marked by major events like the nationalization of banks, the Green Revolution, and the imposition of Emergency, making her both a transformative and controversial leader.

6. Morarji Desai (1977–1979)

Summary: As the first non-Congress Prime Minister, Morarji Desai led India during a time of political change. His government focused on civil liberties, economic liberalization, and reducing central government power, although his tenure was short-lived.

7. Charan Singh (1979–1980)

Summary: Charan Singh, known as a leader of the farmers, served as Prime Minister for a brief period. His tenure was marked by efforts to address rural issues and agricultural reforms, but his government collapsed due to lack of majority support.

8. Indira Gandhi (1980–1984)

Summary: Indira Gandhi's second term saw a mix of economic challenges, social unrest, and significant political events, including Operation Blue Star and her subsequent assassination. Her leadership style remained assertive, and her legacy continues to influence Indian politics.

9. Rajiv Gandhi (1984–1989)

Summary: Rajiv Gandhi, the youngest Prime Minister of India, initiated major technological and economic reforms aimed at modernizing India. His tenure was also marked by challenges, including the Bofors scandal and rising communal tensions.

10. Vishwanath Pratap Singh (1989–1990)

Summary: V. P. Singh is remembered for his focus on social justice, particularly his decision to implement the Mandal Commission's recommendations for reservations in government jobs for OBCs. His tenure was marked by social upheaval and political instability.

11. Chandra Shekhar (1990–1991)

Summary: Chandra Shekhar led a minority government during a period of economic crisis and political uncertainty. His brief tenure focused on economic stabilization and maintaining political order.

12. P. V. Narasimha Rao (1991–1996)

Summary: P. V. Narasimha Rao's leadership marked a turning point in India's economic history with the liberalization reforms of 1991. His government is credited with steering India out of an economic crisis and laying the foundation for modern economic growth.

13. Atal Bihari Vajpayee (1996)

Summary: Vajpayee's first term as Prime Minister lasted only 13 days due to lack of majority support, but it set the stage for his later return as a key figure in Indian politics.

14. H. D. Deve Gowda (1996–1997)

Summary: Deve Gowda, a leader from Karnataka, served as Prime Minister during a period of coalition politics. His government focused on rural development and federalism but was short-lived due to coalition instability.

15. I. K. Gujral (1997–1998)

Summary: I. K. Gujral is remembered for the "Gujral Doctrine," a set of foreign policy principles focused on strengthening India's relations with its neighbors. His tenure, marked by coalition politics, aimed at maintaining domestic stability and improving international relations.

16. Atal Bihari Vajpayee (1998–2004)

Summary: Vajpayee's second term as Prime Minister is notable for significant achievements such as economic reforms, infrastructure development, and nuclear tests in 1998. His leadership also saw efforts to improve Indo-Pakistani relations and enhance India's global stature.

17. Dr. Manmohan Singh (2004–2014)

Summary: Dr. Manmohan Singh's tenure is known for continued economic growth, major social welfare programs, and policy reforms. His administration faced challenges such as corruption scandals but is credited with maintaining economic stability and pursuing social justice.

18. Narendra Modi (2014–Present)

Summary: Narendra Modi's tenure has been marked by significant reforms, including the introduction of the Goods and Services Tax (GST), demonetization, and a strong focus on national security, economic development, and digital innovation. His leadership continues to shape India's trajectory in both domestic and international arenas.

These summaries encapsulate the major aspects of each leader's tenure, highlighting their contributions, challenges, and legacies.

Do You Know About: Presidents of USA 1789 - 2024 by Aryak Singh Chauhan.